RAJASTHAN RISING

A PARTNERSHIP FOR STRONGER INSTITUTIONS AND MORE LIVABLE CITIES

Manoj Sharma and Melissa Alipalo

FEBRUARY 2021

ADB

ASIAN DEVELOPMENT BANK

Notes:
In this publication, "$" refers to United States dollars and "₹" refers to Indian rupees.
All photographs, unless otherwise credited, were taken by Amit Verma.

Cover photo. Investments in hospitals in the ADB-supported Rajasthan Urban Infrastructure Development Project have had catalytic and transformational impacts. Photo shows Meena Damor, medical doctor at Chandpol Satellite District Hospital, a local hospital in Udaipur city and among those upgraded during the first phase of the project. Read more about the impacts of the hospital investments on access to medical services in the "Hospitals" section of this publication (starting on p. 98).

ADB investments in urban hospitals in Rajasthan also helped people like Bimla Devi, 25, who traveled 174 kilometers to the Jon Lone hospital for the urgent care she needed in giving birth to her first child. Her child received care in the new neonatal intensive care unit, and her family rested in the new extensive family waiting room.

CONTENTS

FIGURES AND IMPACT STORIES

FOREWORD

The Government of Rajasthan established the Rajasthan Urban Infrastructure Development Project (RUIDP) as a special purpose vehicle in 1998 for the implementation of urban infrastructure development projects funded by the Asian Development Bank (ADB). It gives me great satisfaction that these projects have benefited the urban population of Rajasthan immensely through their improvements of our drinking water and sewerage systems, in addition to other infrastructure works. The Rajasthan project has now become a renowned name in the field of urban infrastructure development.

RUIDP, in partnership with ADB, has completed 20 glorious years, and it has indeed been a marvelous journey for sustainable urban development. Under various loan assistance projects, more than 30 towns have benefited from infrastructure works totaling more than $1 billion. Moving further toward inclusive growth, the Government of Rajasthan anticipates ADB's support for a fourth phase of the project, which will assist the state government in its ambition to invest further, over time, in 42 towns, with populations of 50,000 to 1 million, including 10 smaller heritage towns, for a total beneficiary population of approximately 3 million. These investments will aim to provide better, sustainable drinking water and sanitation facilities.

Rajasthan Rising offers a glimpse into the ADB–RUIDP partnership, which will continue to provide sustainable development through future projects. I am hopeful that this meticulously prepared publication will succeed in highlighting the mission, the work, and the accomplishments of RUIDP during its journey over 2 decades.

ASHOK GEHLOT
Chief Minister
Government of Rajasthan

FOREWORD

From the Director General, South Asia Department, ADB

The Asian Development Bank (ADB) and the Government of Rajasthan are celebrating more than 20 years of a partnership that has brought sustainable development to the cities and towns of Rajasthan, in northwest India.

This publication will be especially valuable for city and state officials seriously looking for a model that will bring transformative development to their cities and towns. It is a practical and aspirational retrospective of one of ADB's first large-scale, multisector urban development investments in India, the Rajasthan Urban Infrastructure Development Project (RUIDP). Cities and towns across the state have faced challenges typical of urban areas, but they have done so under unusually extreme conditions due to a harsh climate, poverty, and infrastructure deficits.

The Rajasthan project has brought water to some of India's most parched cities. The first and second phases of the program brought a few hours of water supply per day to cities that only had a few hours of water supply *per week*. The third phase of the investment program has begun to provide water to cities 24/7, along with wastewater collection and sewage treatment. Over the 20 years of partnership with ADB, RUIDP has gained experience in more specialized sectors of urban development than perhaps any other single institution in the country, including work on heritage restoration, hospital construction, roads, bridges, water supply, drainage, and sanitation. In recent years, RUIDP has begun to focus on water supply, drainage, and sewerage—realizing that this was how it could make the greatest contribution to our cities. Now, the program has completed two phases, is implementing a third, and preparing for a fourth.

This report highlights the factors of program design, implementation, and evaluation that have helped RUIDP to strengthen over time. Lessons learned during each phase, and applied to the next, are explained in this publication and can be adopted and adapted elsewhere.

Urban planners and decision makers in cities and states across India should value RUIDP as a source of technical assistance, benefiting not only from the program's expertise, especially in procurement, but also in pro-poor design and implementation, project management, and public communications. The practical information in this main report is validated by impact stories that demonstrate the effectiveness of corporate-modeled, pro-poor urban development.

As this report was in its final publishing phase, the coronavirus disease (COVID-19) pandemic had shuttered entire economies, sending billions of people indoors to protect themselves from infection, especially in densely populated cities. The kind of development partnership that ADB and the state government have built is more important than ever as a way to bring much-needed urban development, especially in water and wastewater services and public health. We are working together for more resilient cities. We congratulate the state government and RUIDP on more than 20 years of developing more livable urban areas, with the project continuing to evolve as a model for India's aspiring municipalities. ADB is committed to continuing its support for the state of Rajasthan in its pursuit of healthier, cleaner, and more prosperous towns and cities.

KENICHI YOKOYAMA
Director General
South Asia Department, ADB

FOREWORD

From the Director General, Sustainable Development and
Climate Change Department, ADB

In many ways, the Rajasthan Urban Infrastructure Development Project (RUIDP) was ahead of its time when it was conceptualized in the late 1990s. While rural areas were still dominating the national development agenda in India, the Government of Rajasthan embarked on a $250 million investment with the Asian Development Bank (ADB) in *urban* development, becoming a trailblazer and leader in that field.

The Rajasthan project pursued multisector development to ensure a positive impact on urban economies, on the environment, and on social equity across the state. It has also actively promoted the enablers of sustainable development: strong institutions, reforms, capacity building, and participation, in addition to infrastructure investments. Savings, as well as loan disbursements when the project had reached policy milestones, were reinvested in urban development, proving the state government's independent commitment to sustainable urban development. The approach that ADB and the state government took in designing and implementing RUIDP demonstrates what ADB now promotes as "Livable Cities," a strategy that guides its urban operations across the Asia and Pacific region. Livable Cities reflects years of operational experience in working with a variety of urban development models.

The livable—and survivable—city is an urgent development priority now and in the coming post-COVID-19 world. As this publication goes to press, much of the world is only beginning to cautiously and slowly emerge from months of sheltering in place. For the poor, that "place" has meant congested, poorly ventilated, and poorly serviced slums. With more than half the world's population living in cities, urban centers have taken on new roles. They are no longer just destinations of opportunity and engines of growth, but are now on the frontlines of defense against infectious disease. COVID-19 is a wake-up call, alerting us to the need for more resilient urban design and economies that are intolerant of inequalities and environmental compromises. Investments should clearly be directed toward improving the quality of public health, water and sanitation services, digital connectivity, and the government's capacity to coordinate responses to emergencies.

ADB is proud to share this report on how RUIDP exemplifies the Livable Cities approach. ADB's Strategy 2030 identifies "making cities more livable" as one of seven operational priorities.[*] Its companion document, the *Livable Cities Operational Priority Plan, 2019–2024*, sets out ADB's support for the developing member countries (DMCs), as it has done in Rajasthan, in their efforts to build livable cities by (i) improving the accessibility, quality, and reliability of urban services; (ii) strengthening urban planning and financial sustainability; and (iii) improving urban environments, climate resilience, and disaster management.[†] The plan also helps DMCs develop the right institutions, policies, and enabling environments.

---

[*]   ADB. 2018. *Strategy 2030: Achieving a Prosperous, Inclusive, Resilient, and Sustainable Asia and the Pacific.* Manila.
[†]   ADB. 2019. *Strategy 2030 Operational Plan for Priority 4: Making Cities More Livable, 2019–2024.* Manila.

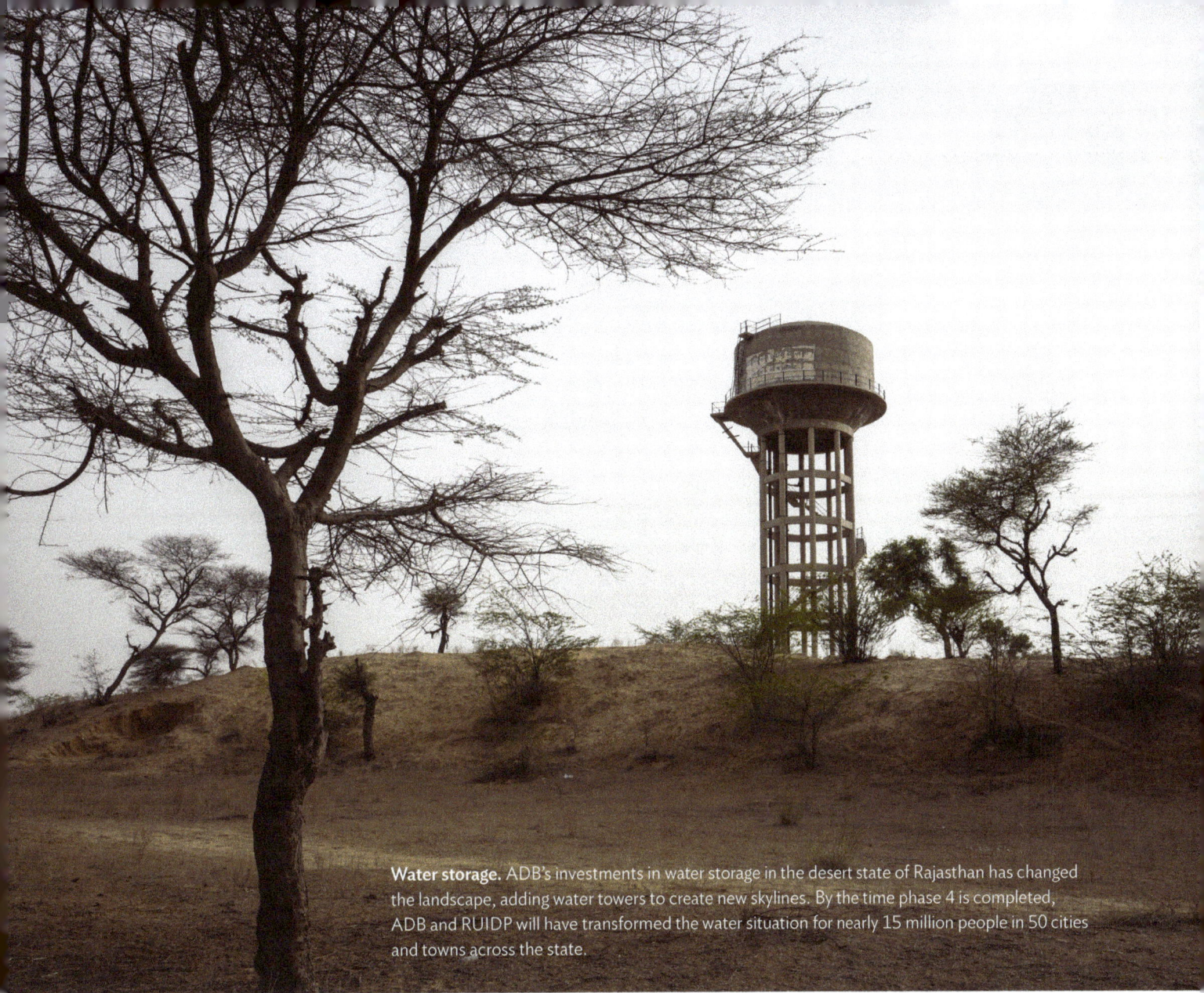

Water storage. ADB's investments in water storage in the desert state of Rajasthan has changed the landscape, adding water towers to create new skylines. By the time phase 4 is completed, ADB and RUIDP will have transformed the water situation for nearly 15 million people in 50 cities and towns across the state.

As this report rightly states, "The results of the RUIDP–ADB partnership exemplify ADB's strategic vision of 'livable cities,' which puts the well-being of people and community at the center of decision-making for urban development." This report is a practical and aspirational case study on how to design, implement, and manage livable cities.

We congratulate the State Government of Rajasthan, RUIDP, and our colleagues in the South Asia Urban Development and Water Division on more than 20 years spent developing more livable cities in Rajasthan and evolving into a model partnership. We remain committed to supporting our DMCs and operational partners in their pursuit of more livable cities.

WOOCHONG UM
Director General
Sustainable Development and Climate Change Department, ADB

ACKNOWLEDGMENTS

This publication is a collaboration between the Asian Development Bank (ADB) and the Rajasthan Urban Infrastructure Development Project (RUIDP), the institutional body now mandated through the newly established Rajasthan Urban Drinking Water, Sewerage & Infrastructure Corporation to implement large-scale international and national investments in urban areas of the state of Rajasthan, India.

Within ADB, this publication is a joint endeavor of the South Asia Urban Development and Water Division (SAUW) and the Urban Sector Group. Manoj Sharma, currently the chief of the Urban Sector Group in ADB's Sustainable Development and Climate Change Department and formerly the project team leader for the ADB-financed urban development projects in Rajasthan while working for SAUW, led the development of this publication, with the support of SAUW Director Norio Saito, SAUW Unit Head of Project Administration Neeta Pokhrel, and Senior Urban Development Specialist Vivian Castro-Wooldridge. Sharma's unique history with the investment program—first as an RUIDP project director and then as SAUW principal urban specialist—provided the editorial team with unique perspectives and access to other knowledge holders. The report team is especially grateful to Sekhar Bonu, who at the time of the initiation of this report was the director of SAUW, for his insights on institutional development and his vision for this publication. Pushkar Srivastava and Ashok Srivastava, both senior urban project officers at the ADB India Resident Mission, participated in extensive interviews; Pushkar Srivastava peer reviewed this report.

RUIDP officials and staff provided guidance and feedback on the report, with support from their consultants and contractors. Former Project Director Jitendra Kr. Soni provided support for the finalization of the publication, and former RUIDP Project Director Preetam Yashvant provided the editorial team with access to staff and project sites during the extensive fieldwork. Special appreciation is due to Suresh Gupta and Babulal Sharma for coordinating and accompanying the editorial team throughout the fieldwork, offering background on project implementation and impacts, and making introductions to key stakeholders. Gupta also provided a comprehensive summary of many lessons and good practices featured in this report, and helped gather and confirm additional information needed to finalize the document during the difficulties of the COVID-19 lockdown. The editorial team is indebted to government officials, elected representatives, and RUIDP engineers and consultants interviewed for this publication.

The editorial team was composed of Melissa Howell Alipalo (researcher, writer, and editorial director), Amit Verma (photographer), and Gaurav Sharma (knowledge specialist). They traveled across Rajasthan twice to document the impacts of RUIDP. All photographs, unless otherwise credited, were taken by Amit Verma. They are especially indebted to the beneficiaries of RUIDP's investments for courageously sharing their homes and stories with ADB and RUIDP. They showed great hope and resilience amid their adversity, uncertainty, and vulnerability. The respect that RUIDP staff and consultants showed to project communities is a testimony of their diligence and enhances the credibility of their good reputation.

The publication was edited by Joanne Gerber, proofread by Lawrence Casiraya, page proof checked by Corazon Desuasido, and typeset by Alvin Tubio. The ADB Department of Communications provided valuable guidance on ADB's publishing standards and procedures.

REPORT PREPARATION CORE TEAM

Manoj Sharma is currently the chief of the Urban Sector Group in ADB's Sustainable Development and Climate Change Department and formerly the project team leader for the ADB-financed urban development projects in Rajasthan, while working in ADB's South Asia Urban Development and Water Division.

WRITER AND PUBLICATION COORDINATOR
Melissa Howell Alipalo

PHOTOGRAPHER
Amit Verma

KNOWLEDGE SPECIALIST
Gaurav Sharma

PEER REVIEWER
Pushkar Srivastava

EDITOR
Joanne Gerber

TYPESETTER
Alvin Tubio

ABBREVIATIONS

ADB	Asian Development Bank
AMRUT	Atal Mission for Rejuvenation and Urban Transformation
CAPP	Community Awareness and Participation Program
DMA	district metered area
DMC	developing member country
DSC	design supervision consultant
FSM	fecal sludge management
GSDP	gross state domestic product
IAS	Indian Administrative Service
JWSSB	Jaipur Water Supply and Sewerage Board
m³	cubic meter
MLD	million liters per day (or megaliter per day)
NGO	nongovernment organization
O&M	operation and maintenance
PHED	Public Health Engineering Department
PIU	project implementation unit
PMC	project management consultant
PMU	project management unit
ROB	rail over bridge
RUDSICO	Rajasthan Urban Drinking Water, Sewerage & Infrastructure Corporation
RUIDP	Rajasthan Urban Infrastructure Development Project
SIP	service improvement program
ULB	urban local body

FROM THE EXECUTING AGENCY

"One reason why the Rajasthan Urban Infrastructure Development Program (RUIDP) is so commendable is that, since it was established, the leadership and staff have always pushed for new and better ways to modernize our urban infrastructure. They looked beyond the boundaries of what they knew and the standards here in India. They looked to communities and stakeholders through consultations, to understand the communities' needs, priorities, and capacities, believing that a consumer welfare approach was best. They looked for best practices across the world, and believed that those ideas could be applied here. And they were right to do so. I believe that they'll continue to innovate because technologies are rapidly evolving, especially in sewerage and water supply, which Rajasthan needs to be very smart about."

—SHANTI KUMAR DHARIWAL
Minister, Urban Development and Housing and Local Self Government, Rajasthan

"Other states and municipalities should look to Rajasthan and RUIDP for technical assistance in urban development. RUIDP is a center of excellence, and what makes it so unique is the commitment and experience of its professionals. RUIDP, from the beginning, seemed to know that professionalism would make the difference. It had an institutional value that it instilled in everything it did, and communities are benefiting because of it."

—BHAWANI SINGH DETHA
(India Administrative Service) Secretary,
Local Self Government Department, Rajasthan

EXECUTIVE SUMMARY

The Asian Development Bank (ADB) and the Government of Rajasthan recently crossed a threshold of more than 20 years of partnership in bringing sustainable development to the cities and towns of Rajasthan, in northwest India. This retrospective of the 2-decade journey of the Rajasthan Urban Infrastructure Development Project (RUIDP) was intended first and foremost as a model of good urban development and project management practices. It was also intended as a celebration of the project's extraordinary results.

During the final stages of the preparation of this publication, the coronavirus disease (COVID-19) was spreading across the world. ADB, the state government, and all those involved in RUIDP intended this report to be a meditation and call to action, a call to envision the post-COVID-19 city, especially the institutions that will need to have greater resiliency. With half of the world's population living in cities, which fuel most national economies and poverty reduction strategies, we cannot help but review and present the story of Rajasthan's urban development through the COVID-19 lens. The lessons and results of RUIDP were and continue to be hard-won, which makes it an ideal case study for the economic rebuilding and new opportunities that cities had been enjoying, and that they will now have to fight hard to recover.

In 1998, ADB and the state government embarked on an investment program that set a new benchmark for ADB's urban operations in South Asia. RUIDP pioneered urban development on a statewide scale, with institutional strengthening at its core. From the beginning, both ADB and the state government believed that an autonomous, high-skilled, and well-managed entity with a singular focus on urban infrastructure and governance would be key to successful scale, impact, and sustainability. RUIDP, as an institution, would be their proof of concept.

Certainly, there were easier places in India than Rajasthan for ADB to advance its mission of urban development in the late 1990s. Rajasthan is the driest state in the country, much of it desert and scrubland, and divided by mountains and ravines. It is the largest state in India, claiming 10% of the country's total land area (some 340,000 square kilometers, about the size of Germany). In place of Rajasthan's famed, but fallen princely kingdoms, cities have risen—233 of them—wherever the climate, water resources, and soil fertility were most conducive. And it was here that a showcase of urban development, rooted in institutional development, has emerged for other Indian states and municipal governments to consider and adapt.

After 20 years of experience in design, implementation, and monitoring, RUIDP has benefited from lessons learned and good practices acquired from one end of the state to the other, which illustrates the benefits of good urban development and strong institution building. This publication attempts to consolidate the knowledge accumulated during the project's history through interviews with beneficiaries and other key stakeholders from ADB, RUIDP, and the state government. The comprehensiveness of this publication requires a reader who is seriously interested in urban development and institution building in India's cities.

The publication is organized into four chapters presenting the issues, solutions, and results of the ADB–RUIDP partnership. In the introductory chapter, "Issues: Developing Urban Deserts," the report outlines the geo-environmental, socioeconomic landscape of Rajasthan and its cities. The second chapter, "Solutions: Good Urban Development Practices," the primary purpose of this report, providing a practical tour, project phase by project phase, of the good practices and lessons learned that RUIDP's project management has adopted over the years. The third chapter, "Results: More Livable Cities," uses ADB's policy framework of Livable Cities to examine the results of RUIDP. The fourth chapter, "Unfinished Business: The Next Phase," looks at how remaining challenges need to be addressed to further strengthen the program.

Issues: Developing Urban Deserts

To appreciate the development challenges confronting Rajasthan at the outset of the investment program, ADB examined the environmental, social, and economic landscape of the state in the late 1990s, and later how it developed over the course of the RUIDP phases. It found that a deficit of infrastructure and capacity had constrained the development of Rajasthan's cities and towns.

In the state's harsh economic landscape, ADB established itself in 1998, when it initiated RUIDP with a loan of $250 million, to be invested in six divisional headquarter cities. RUIDP was ADB's second large-scale urban program in India, after the successful completion of a program in the state of Karnataka; there was a city-level effort getting underway in Kolkata.

ADB and the state government both envisioned strong institution-led development and diverse urban initiatives in Rajasthan. RUIDP would be a full-fledged institution, not a typical project management office tucked away in a corner of some government building, with its leadership and staff dividing their time between the project and their regular government duties. Instead, RUIDP was intended to become a permanent, corporatized institution devoted to securing investments in urban development in the state, and to facilitating the design, implementation, and management of those investments.

Solutions: Good Urban Development Practices

What distinguishes RUIDP as a project management entity is its ability to incorporate lessons into its daily and systematic practices over a long operational period. This continuous institutional strengthening has fostered a corporate culture that treats efficiency and quality as a double bottom line. The ADB–RUIDP partnership exemplifies the key principles and practices that ADB encourages its operational staff to adhere to when designing investments for more livable cities (and which this chapter explores): investing in strategic zones and corridors rather than widely across a country; taking the long view of development; building long-term investment partnerships with government clients; involving the public in urban planning and investment design; and transforming cities with a critical mass of financing and capacity building, rather than just making modest improvements within a single sector of a single city.

The solutions, lessons, and experiences that RUIDP has garnered are presented in this chapter as good practices for other municipalities to follow. The guidelines cover the stages of the project management cycle: selection and design, preparation and implementation, and monitoring and evaluation.

Diverting trouble. ADB investments in the city of Kota, Rajasthan, included the construction of a 5.7-kilometer flood diversion channel. The barrage diverted 540 cubic meters of water from 70 square kilometers of surrounding plateau. The project brought instant relief to the problem of chronic water logging from monsoon rains in Kota.

Many of the good practices are based on capacity building and lessons learned that were incorporated into the design and implementation of subsequent investment phases. The guidance provided during the preparation-and-implementation stage was organized according to the standard aspects of project management: organizational arrangements and principles, financial management, procurement, and implementation.

Results: More Livable Cities

The partnership between RUIDP and ADB is in its third phase and preparing for a fourth phase, having invested nearly $1 billion in 27 cities and the well-being of 10 million people in Rajasthan over more than 20 years. Figure 2, on page 11, summarizes the four phases of RUIDP, showing the sizes of their total investments, scopes of work, benefits, and impacts on people and communities. The final two chapters of this report—"Results: More Livable Cities" and "Unfinished Business: The Next Phase"—look more closely at the results and impacts of RUIDP across sectors and stakeholder groups, as well as within RUIDP.

The institution that ADB and the state government established to lead the investment program is among the country's best government corporations. RUIDP is a career maker for up-and-coming engineers, specialists, and contractors, as well as for seasoned professionals. RUIDP's experts, systems, and practices have created what ADB staff have dubbed "a development ecosystem."

The results of the RUIDP–ADB partnership exemplify ADB's strategic vision of livable cities which puts the well-being of people and community at the center of decision-making regarding urban development. RUIDP is an elaborate case study in how to design, structure, and manage livable cities. RUIDP's results demonstrate how the partnership's designers were forward thinkers in their pursuit of what ADB has identified as the "5Es" of livable cities:

- **Economic competitiveness**—increased competitiveness of urban areas in Rajasthan, through investments in priority infrastructure (especially water supply systems), urban services, and capacity building for more efficient living, commuting, working, and conduct of business.
- **Environmental sustainability and resilience**—investments in sewerage and drainage systems; in solid waste management; and in climate- and disaster-resilient infrastructure, urban planning, and disaster reduction and preparedness for more adaptable, climate-ready cities.
- **Equity and inclusion**—upgrading of community-based infrastructure and connecting informal users to the main systems, thereby converting them into paying customers of urban services; improvements in access to health services; rehabilitation of community assets (ponds, heritage sites, and parks); and the involvement of marginalized groups in planning, implementation, and monitoring.
- **Enabling environment**—a strengthened enabling environment through institutional development and capacity building by RUIDP, urban local bodies (ULBs), line agencies, executing agencies, etc., also through policy reforms and stronger urban governance, for more integrated planning and financial sustainability.
- **Engagement**—greater engagement by the public achieved by mainstreaming and mandating consultations, raising awareness, and involving public participation as standard operating procedures of RUIDP throughout the project cycle, thus successfully demonstrating RUIDP's value to contractors and engineers, who have subsequently participated in non-RUIDP projects.

Project Impact Stories

To illustrate the impacts of the ADB–RUIDP investments on the poor, vignettes ("Impact Stories") that highlight lessons learned, good practices, and achieved results are embedded throughout the report to offer a glimpse of RUIDP's challenges, and what they have meant to the institution and the people it serves.

The investments in slums, hospitals, solid waste systems, and fire stations were relatively small—just 6% of the total program cost for phase 1, yet their value may have been greater than the numbers show because many of these smaller investments served as catalysts for more ambitious ones.

The larger investments in new water system connections inspired the poor residents to invest in their homes. RUIDP provided leverage for hospitals to secure more funds for a further expansion of their facilities and services, so they could serve more people, especially from the poorer outskirts of urban areas. Women felt empowered when given a seat at a table, a microphone at a consultation, and a role in a project. And some communities are asking, "What's next?" That is because infrastructure development and empowerment have the positive tendency to raise expectations.

Urban desert in Rajasthan. The far western Thar Desert border town of Jaisalmer is an iconic example of Rajasthan's arid urban landscapes. Jaisalmer's ancient relics may beckon tourists, but its urban sprawl reflects the city's anxious quest for modernity and economic growth.

ISSUES
DEVELOPING URBAN DESERTS

In 1998, the Asian Development Bank (ADB) and the Government of Rajasthan embarked on an investment program that set a new benchmark for ADB's urban operations in South Asia. The Rajasthan Urban Infrastructure Development Project (RUIDP) pioneered urban development on a statewide scale, with institutional strengthening at its core. From the beginning, ADB and the state government believed that an autonomous, high-skilled, and well-managed entity with a singular focus on urban infrastructure and governance would be key to successful scale, impact, and sustainability. RUIDP, as an institution, would be their proof of concept.

At the time, Rajasthan was confronting development conditions that still exist in many Indian cities today: less-than-ideal rates of in-migration, population growth, infrastructure deficits, and rising social inequality. Despite these challenges, the development of cities and economic growth are interdependent, so the issues that challenge urban growth or livability need to be figured out.

ADB's current urban development strategy for "livable cities" was decades away from being articulated when RUIDP was first getting off the ground. At the time, the Government of India was still focused on rural development. The pivot came quickly, though, and urban development as an engine for economic growth has been a recognized strategy of the Indian government since the first articulation of the concept in its Tenth Five-Year Plan, 2002–2007. The government put monetary muscle behind the strategy with a number of programs, such as the Jawaharlal Nehru National Urban Renewal Mission and its subcomponent, the Urban Infrastructure Development Scheme for Small and Medium Towns.

> Cities are never finished developing, and the COVID-19 pandemic has sounded a wake-up call, signaling the urgent need for urban investments to protect public health and safety and to strengthen economic resiliency.

RUIDP and ADB have accrued more than 20 years of experience in implementing an aggressive urban development agenda. The partnership has not been without its challenges, but RUIDP's decisive leadership, swift corrective actions, and assimilation of lessons learned demonstrated the viability of institution-focused urban development and project management.

Cities are never finished developing, and the COVID-19 pandemic has sounded a wake-up call, signaling the urgent need for investments in urban water supply and sanitation, safe housing, smart city solutions, and urban governance—to protect public health and safety and to strengthen economic resiliency. The ADB–RUIDP partnership has accrued a critical mass of investments, experience, and knowledge that it can share with other states and municipalities interested in achieving better quality urban life. In this introductory chapter, "Issues: Developing Urban Deserts," the report outlines the context for RUIDP's work: the geo-environmental and socioeconomic conditions of Rajasthan and its cities. The second chapter, "Solutions: Good Urban Development Practices," the primary objective of this report, provides a practical tour, project phase by project phase, of the good practices and lessons learned that RUIDP's project management has adopted over the years. The third chapter of the report, "Results: More Livable Cities," uses ADB's policy framework of livable cities to examine the results of RUIDP. The concluding chapter, "Unfinished Business: The Next Phase," offers examples of project impacts, lessons learned, and good practices that are representative of RUIDP's struggles and triumphs since 2000.

Desert landscapes. This view of Jaipur, the capital city of Rajasthan, and of the surrounding arid landscape, is typical of many cities in the state.

The Landscape

A fundamental problem that cities in Rajasthan face is the lack of water.

Rajasthan is the driest state in the country. The Aravalli Mountain Range slices the state diagonally and casts a rain shadow over 60% of the state's western region, where the Thar Desert forms a natural border with Pakistan. The Aravalli's rain shadow limits western Rajasthan to only about 400 millimeters of rain in an average year, which is how much eastern Rajasthan will get in just 11 days of average rain, making it far more fertile, hospitable, populated, and prosperous.

Rajasthan is not endowed with the water resources that cities, economies, and populations require. It is the largest state in the country, covering 10% of India's total land area, and accounting for 5% of its population, but with only about 1% of the country's surface water resources and 1.7% of the country's groundwater.[1] Studies have shown that Rajasthan experiences some of the greatest climate sensitivity in the country, having the highest incidence of drought nationally and a low adaptive capacity. The 20th century saw 48 drought years of varying intensity, putting Rajasthan's chance of a meteorological drought at 47%.

---

[1]   International Finance Corporation (IFC). 2013. *Rajasthan Water Assessment: Potential for Private Sector Investments.* New Delhi.

Strewn across Rajasthan's landscapes are renowned archaeological and architectural relics, attracting tourists and their foreign currency. Of India's certified and protected heritage sites, 25% are found in Rajasthan. The hilltop remains of stone forts are imposing features across the landscape, with fortress walls that stretch beyond visibility in some places. Inside the many forts and palaces are the curated treasures of princes who once had much to defend. Rajasthan cannot afford to leave its history in the past. There is too much profitability, employment, and investment potential in tourism, and there are amenities in the cities near these sites. See Impact Story 1 on the effects of a natural and human-made water crisis on a city's tourism industry, and how water engineering has alleviated the crisis.

Impact Story 1

Udaipur: Water Engineering Rescues a City's Tourism Economy

The southern border city of Udaipur is an oasis in Rajasthan's desert landscape.

The City of Lakes sits amid 10 ancient human-made lakes on the southern slope of the Aravalli Range, fortunately on the monsoon side of the mountains. Udaipur is one of India's most popular tourist destinations. Over 1.4 million tourists visited the city in 2016, almost triple the local population. Its world-renowned luxury hotels and resorts have hosted Hollywood and Bollywood stars and movie sets.

Damage to water-reliant tourism. One of Udaipur's most iconic destinations is the famed Taj Lake Palace hotel, situated at the center of Udaipur's Lake Pichola, where it seems to float majestically on the water. It is reachable only by water taxis, and commands panoramic views of the ancient palaces in the city's lowlands.

So, imagine what happens to a touristy lake city after a decade of light monsoons and decades of extractions from the city's groundwater and surface water supplies that were unsustainable, with no sewerage or solid waste management system. Add to that the deforestation of the surrounding hills. The economy, environment, employment, and, by extension, social development started to unravel. By 2009, the city's centerpiece lake hit rock bottom, literally. It dried up completely, and the city lost its primary source of drinking water. Udaipur's tourism industry was gutted. Where boats once ferried deep-pocketed tourists across Lake Pichola to Taj Lake Palace, grass was visible, attracting wild horses from the surrounding hills, while buffalo ambled in from the plains to lounge around the puddles that remained at the bottom of the abandoned lake. Impromptu cricket matches took place on the lake bottom as well, according to media reports at the time.

Were it not for the innovative engineering of the eighth century, Udaipur would have likely resembled the rest of Rajasthan: parched. But it was able to draw upon dams and cascading human-made lakes that caught rainwater and distributed it throughout the city. This time, however, even this proved to be no match for 20th century urbanization, inadequate infrastructure, the lack of a modern water management system, and local climate variations.

An engineering challenge. Asian Development Bank (ADB) financing and the ingenuity of the Rajasthan Urban Infrastructure Development Project (RUIDP) have together brought relief to Udaipur's environment and economy. The construction of the Mansi Wakal Dam (a joint venture of Hindustan Zinc Ltd. and the Public Health and Engineering Department) applied standard engineering and construction methods to reduce the water deficit in the city and the local aquifers. The real engineering feat came in laying the pipeline across 30 kilometers of rocky, winding hills between the dam site, in Gorana village, and the city. The highest ridge along the most convenient route for the pipeline was 1,100 meters. This would have required about five pumps and high recurring energy costs for the city. But engineers love a good challenge. Why go over the ridge, when you can go through it? RUIDP contractor Valecha Engineering bore a 4.5-kilometer tunnel through the mountain to enable the water flow.

continued on next page

Water-reliant urban tourism. Udaipur's famed Taj Lake Palace hotel is a centerpiece of tourism in Udaipur and Lake Pichola, which dried up completely from both natural and human-made causes, such as years of lighter monsoon and over extraction from the lake for the city's water supply. The drying lake bed gutted the city's tourism industry. The ADB-financed Mansi Wakal Dam has helped revive the lake, protect the tourist economy, and improve water supplies to the city by 66%.

"The beauty of this project is gravity. There is only one water lifting from the dam. The rest is gravity-fed," said Ram Pal Jingar, executive engineer for RUIDP. He worked as an assistant engineer on the tunnel construction from 2003 to 2008.

The dam now supplies the city with 35 million liters per day (MLD); that has meant an increase in the total water supply by 66%, from 53 MLD to 88 MLD. As a result, the city began to rely less on groundwater, giving the aquifers a chance to replenish the lakes. By the summer of 2018, Lake Pichola was full again.

The ADB-financed Mansi Wakal Dam thus helped to revive the lake, improve Udaipur's water supplies, and save the city's critical tourism economy.

Remaining challenges. The ADB–RUIDP investments may have only bought Udaipur some extra time, however, as the city still needs to boost its water supply by another 53% (47 MLD) if it intends to meet the government's requirement of 135 MLD. It must also invest in sewerage and solid waste management, and in slum improvement, which the original ADB–RUIDP investment proposal had included, but the municipal council refused to borrow for, according to RUIDP staff. The council did accept financing for other key infrastructure projects, such as upgrading the facilities and services of a hospital on the city's underserved outskirts, building a road and bridge that will be critical for improving connectivity in the city, and building a new fire station.

Source: Authors.

The Economy

Rajasthan is a natural corridor between the wealthy northern and western states of India, making it an important center for trade and commerce. Rajasthan's cities contribute around 48% of the gross state domestic product (GSDP), and are projected to contribute more than 60% by 2030.[2] Also, the fast-growing economic sectors in Rajasthan are found mostly in the urban areas. However, the services sector, which includes the tourism industry (especially important for Rajasthan), contributes only about 44% of GSDP, below the national average of 54%.

Tourism in Rajasthan accounts for 9% to the GSDP.[3] In 2018, there were 50 million domestic visitors to the state, double the figure in 2010,[4] and there were 1.5 million foreign visitors. Rajasthan ranks third nationally in domestic tourist arrivals and sixth in foreign tourist arrivals.[5] Tourism employs directly or indirectly 890,000 people, or 3% of the state's total population.[6] With $275.5 billion in tourism revenues in 2018 and a growth rate of 9.4%, it holds great potential for Rajasthan.

The Cities

In the 1990s, a quarter of the state's population lived in cities, and the migration rate was putting pressure on the already weak urban infrastructure. The productivity rate of cities was 3.5 times higher than in rural areas. The most recent census (2011) counted 68.6 million people in Rajasthan, with 25% of them living in 193 urban centers. From 2001 to 2011, the total urban population grew at a rate of 25%, and the population growth rate within the cities was 29%, compared with 19% in rural areas during the same decade. Though the urban growth rate has been strong, Rajasthan still remains less urbanized than other states. Infrastructure investments will be key to making cities hospitable for migrants, making them easier places in which to do business, and reducing the poverty there.

---

[2] S. Sankhe et al. 2010. *India's Urban Awakening: Building Inclusive Cities, Sustaining Economic Growth.* New Delhi: McKinsey Global Institute.

[3] World Bank. 2018. *Rajasthan Playing to Its Strengths: A Strategy for Sustained and Inclusive Growth.* Washington, DC. The poverty line is a measurement and poverty threshold used by the Indian government to indicate economic disadvantage and to identify individuals and households in need of government assistance.

[4] Government of Rajasthan. *Tourism Department Annual Progress Report 2018–19* (in Hindi). Jaipur.

[5] Government of India, Ministry of Tourism. 2016. *India Tourism Statistics 2015.* New Delhi. Cited in World Bank. 2018. *Rajasthan Playing to Its Strengths: A Strategy for Sustained and Inclusive Growth.* Washington, DC.

[6] These estimates are from an economic impact analysis presented in: Government of India, Ministry of Tourism: *Regional Tourism Satellite Account Rajasthan, 2009–10, National Council of Applied Economic Research.* New Delhi. Cited in World Bank, *Rajasthan Playing to Its Strengths.*

Figure 1: Rajasthan Poverty Estimates, 1993–2013
(%)

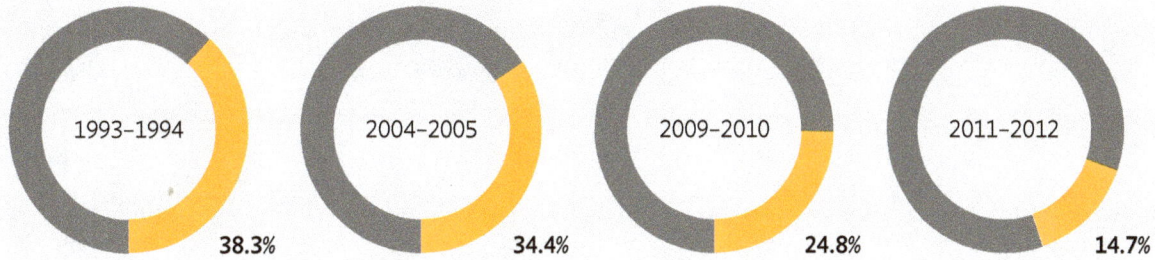

1993–1994   **38.3%**
2004–2005   **34.4%**
2009–2010   **24.8%**
2011–2012   **14.7%**

Source: Government of India, Ministry of Statistics and Programme Implementation, National Sample Survey Office.

The Poor

Poverty rates have been falling across the state since 1993, most significantly since 2004 (Figure 1). In 2004, when the ADB investments were in the early years of their implementation, the statewide poverty rate was estimated at 34%.[7] According to the 2011 census, the proportion of the population living below the poverty line was 16%; in the cities, it was 11%.

Development organizations have published much higher figures for the poor and slum populations in Rajasthan, for instance reporting that 24.8% of the population were living below the poverty line in 2013 (footnote 1). Moreover, even a marginally higher poverty line would raise the poverty rate significantly, as a large part of the population is clustered just above the official poverty line.

The 2011 census recorded the slum population as 3% of the total population of Rajasthan, with the 2011 urban slum residents at 9.8% of the total urban population.[8] Based on measures of per capita consumption expenditure,[9] inequality held steady during 2004–2005 to 2009–2010, and the state's rates of inequality were actually lower than in most other low-income states (footnote 8). Rajasthan still ranks low among the country's poorest states, however, when it comes to social development indicators on health, education, and quality of life. Benefits provided under the National Food Security Act are distributed to 54% of Rajasthan's urban population and to 69% of its rural population (footnote 8).

Rajasthan's towns and cities have always been among the best-planned in India, but rapid population growth since around 1970 has created new kinds and depths of poverty. The decade-long population growth rate is 21.44%, one of the country's highest. Per capita income is $1,122, which is below the country's average.

---

[7]   World Bank. 2018. *Rajasthan Playing to Its Strengths*.

[8]   Government of Rajasthan. 2015. *A Report of Task Force on Elimination of Poverty*. Jaipur.

[9]   The Indian government gauges inequalities using the Gini coefficient method for measuring the distribution of wealth, as indicated by per capita consumption expenditure. The Rajasthan Task Force on Elimination of Poverty noted in a 2015 report that consumption inequality underestimates poverty, and that a better indicator of poverty rates is household income.

Infrastructure gap. A woman on the outskirts of Udaipur refills a disposable plastic bottle with water that has leaked from the pipeline carrying water to the city proper, a reminder of the infrastructure gap just outside the city limits.

The Challenge

Cities across India need an estimated $1.2 trillion per year for infrastructure development.[10] A study by the state government determined that the urban water supply alone in Rajasthan would need a capital investment of $4.5 billion from 2015 to 2030 for the rehabilitation and augmentation of various urban water schemes.[11] To put this figure into perspective, ADB's investments in the state topped $1 billion after 20 years—and that is less than one-fourth of what the state government said it needed for just 2015–2030.[12]

---

[10]   A 2010 study estimated that India needed $1.2 trillion by 2030 (or $134 per capita per year) for urban infrastructure; the Indian government's High Powered Expert Committee concluded similarly. See S. Sankhe et al., *India's Urban Awakening.*

[11]   SMEC International Pty Limited. 2013. *Benchmarking of Urban Water Supply Schemes of Rajasthan: Final Report.* Jaipur: Government of Rajasthan.

[12]   The Government of Rajasthan estimated that the state's urban water supply would need a capital investment of $4.5 billion over three phases: phase 1 (2015–2020): $1.5 billion; phase 2 (2021–2025): $1.7 billion; and phase 3 (2026–2030): $1.3 billion. Of ADB's nearly $1 billion investment in Rajasthan's urban areas, about 30% has been spent on water supplies.

The required capital investment is far beyond what urban local bodies (ULBs) can afford or mobilize. The private sector is cautiously entering new public infrastructure spaces outside of telecommunication, transportation, aviation, and energy. Public–private partnerships are largely limited to operation and maintenance (O&M) contracts or, to a far less degree, temporary ownership while a company recovers its investment. The potential for both financing and private sector entry is diminished by problems with municipal management and regulations. Political term limits do not align with long-term investment strategies and development horizons. State governments and ULBs are reluctant to levy user charges, so few public services come with any real price tag for users or revenue streams for utilities. Other key sources of revenue— such as property taxes, publicly owned assets (e.g., land), and fees for licenses—remain underutilized.

Development leaders and administrators are coming to terms with what must change and what must be done. Cities are beginning to be understood as socially and economically viable enterprises, providing services to valued, paying customers, whose satisfaction is key to achieving the goals of growth, equitable prosperity, and sustainability.

To harness the state's strategic location and attract investments in its key sectors—such as cement, agriculture and allied industries, and mineral and mineral-processing industries—the state's urban areas needed massive investments in basic infrastructure. In 1998, when RUIDP was just beginning, the state government identified the construction and expansion of key urban infrastructure and services as priorities for achieving the state's development goals. Water supply, sewerage, and drainage were the urban infrastructure priorities.

ADB Support for Rajasthan

In Rajasthan's harsh economic landscape, ADB established itself in 1998, when it initiated RUIDP with a loan of $250 million, to be invested in six divisional headquarter cities. RUIDP was ADB's second large-scale urban investment program in India,[13] after the successful completion of a program in the state of Karnataka; there was a city-level effort getting underway in Kolkata.

ADB and the state government both envisioned strong institution-led development and diverse urban initiatives in Rajasthan. RUIDP would be a full-fledged institution, not a typical project management office tucked away in a corner of some government building, with its leadership and staff dividing their time between the project and their regular government duties. Instead, RUIDP was intended to become a permanent, corporatized institution devoted to securing investments in urban development in the state, and to facilitating the design, implementation, and management of those investments. As a result of policy reforms supported by ADB, RUIDP later merged with other urban institutions to become the Rajasthan Urban Drinking Water, Sewerage & Infrastructure Corporation (RUDSICO), whose founding and development are discussed in various sections of this report. Taking a historical view, but also taking into account RUDSICO's staff, who are directly responsible for the project's water supply and sewerage investments, this report uses the "RUIDP" abbreviation when discussing phases 1–3.

---

[13] Although RUIDP is referred to as a "Project" in its name, it is also referred to as a "program" in this report. That is because it operates at both the program level, in the form of the decision-making done by the state government, and at the project level, in the form of the design, implementation, and supervision by the participating cities. See the subsection, "Manage Both the Program and Project Levels," on page 31.

The Results

The ADB–RUIDP partnership is preparing for the fourth phase of the project, having invested nearly $1 billion in 27 cities to promote the well-being of 10 million people in Rajasthan for over 20 years. ADB invested $250 million to improve access to quality municipal services throughout the state and to make the utilization of the state's scarce water resources more efficient. Phase 4 began implementation in late 2020. During that phase, water supply and sanitation infrastructure investments will focus on secondary towns, and there will be further support for the implementation of the state's reform agenda and for statewide capacity building.

"If you could walk through cities in Rajasthan 20 years ago and then walk through those same cities now, you would see how RUIDP has transformed the urban landscape," said former RUIDP Project Director Jitendra Kumar Soni. "And RUIDP isn't finished yet. There will always be the next city, the next piece of infrastructure to build or improve. RUIDP may be 20 years old, but it is just the beginning of this institution's legacy."

" PROJECT VOICES

If you could walk through cities in Rajasthan 20 years ago and then walk through those same cities now, you would see how RUIDP has transformed the urban landscape.

Jitendra Kumar Soni, former RUIDP project director

The institution that ADB and the state government established to lead the investment project is now among the country's best government corporations. RUIDP is a career maker for up-and-coming engineers, specialists, and contractors, as well as for seasoned professionals. RUIDP's experts, systems, and practices have created what ADB staff have dubbed "a development ecosystem."

Figure 2 summarizes the four phases of RUIDP, showing the sizes of their total investments, scopes of work, benefits, and impacts on people and communities (projected in the case of phase 4 and the project total). The third chapter looks more closely at the results and the impact of RUIDP across sectors and stakeholder groups, as well as within RUIDP.

Figure 2: Brief Overview of the Rajasthan Urban Infrastructure Development Project, 1998–2020

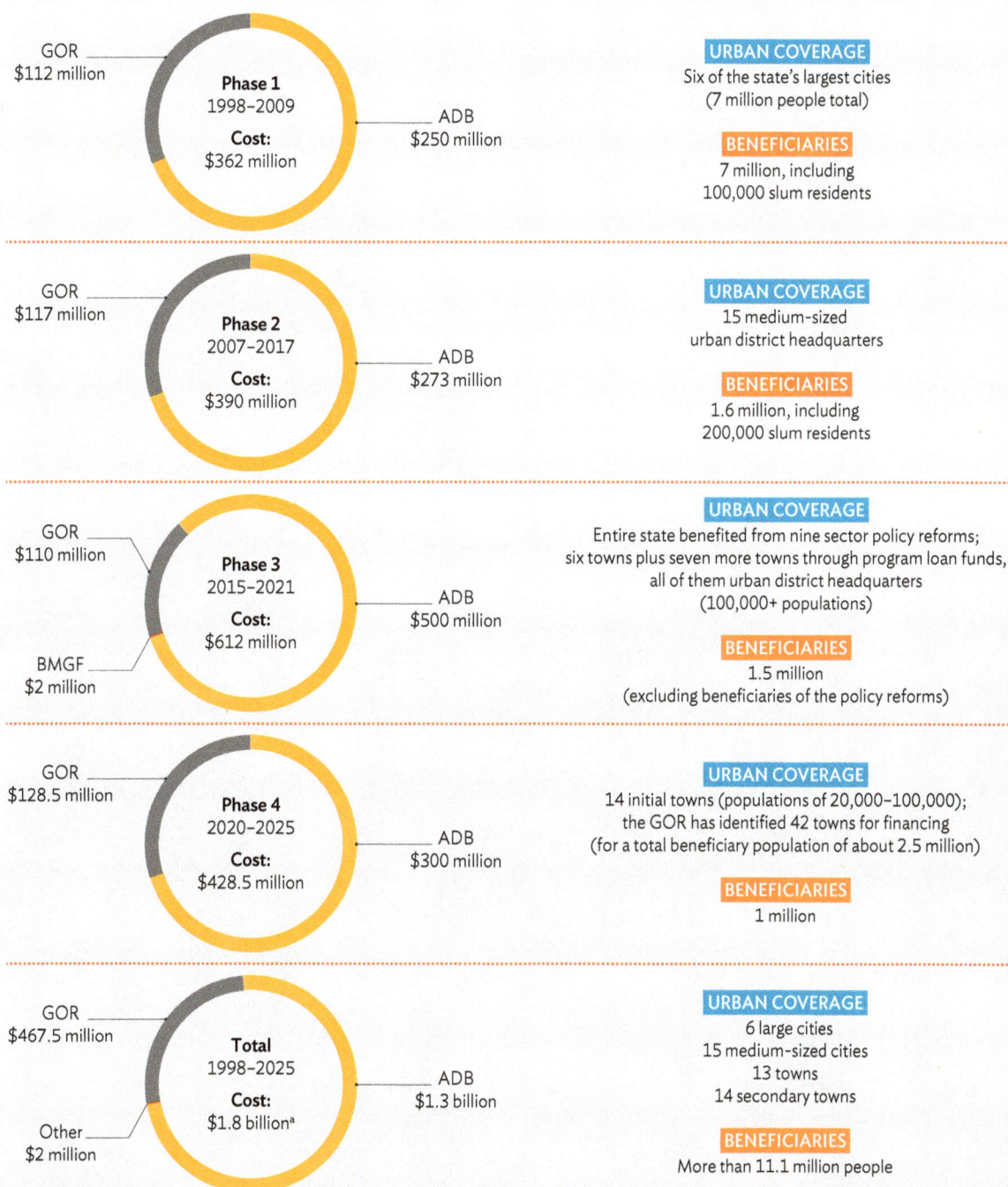

GOR
$112 million

Phase 1
1998–2009
Cost:
$362 million

ADB
$250 million

URBAN COVERAGE
Six of the state's largest cities
(7 million people total)

BENEFICIARIES
7 million, including
100,000 slum residents

GOR
$117 million

Phase 2
2007–2017
Cost:
$390 million

ADB
$273 million

URBAN COVERAGE
15 medium-sized
urban district headquarters

BENEFICIARIES
1.6 million, including
200,000 slum residents

GOR
$110 million

Phase 3
2015–2021
Cost:
$612 million

ADB
$500 million

BMGF
$2 million

URBAN COVERAGE
Entire state benefited from nine sector policy reforms;
six towns plus seven more towns through program loan funds,
all of them urban district headquarters
(100,000+ populations)

BENEFICIARIES
1.5 million
(excluding beneficiaries of the policy reforms)

GOR
$128.5 million

Phase 4
2020–2025
Cost:
$428.5 million

ADB
$300 million

URBAN COVERAGE
14 initial towns (populations of 20,000–100,000);
the GOR has identified 42 towns for financing
(for a total beneficiary population of about 2.5 million)

BENEFICIARIES
1 million

GOR
$467.5 million

Total
1998–2025
Cost:
$1.8 billion[a]

ADB
$1.3 billion

Other
$2 million

URBAN COVERAGE
6 large cities
15 medium-sized cities
13 towns
14 secondary towns

BENEFICIARIES
More than 11.1 million people

BENEFITS

INCREASED ECONOMIC COMPETITIVENESS
– Improved water supply
– Improved roads and bridges
– Restored cultural heritage

INCREASED SOCIAL EQUITY
– Upgraded slums
– New and upgraded hospitals
– New fire stations and
  emergency response vehicles

ENVIRONMENT
– Improved wastewater
  management
– Improved solid waste
  management
– Improved urban drainage

ENABLING
– Capacity development
– Nine policy reforms

ADB = Asian Development Bank, BMGF = Bill & Melinda Gates Foundation, GOR = Government of Rajasthan.

[a] The total here is slightly higher than the sum of the component figures due to rounding.

Source: Authors.

Diversifying the development workforce.
Neelam Meena (left) and Nisha Beniwal (right),
junior engineers with RUIDP, visit a site where
trenches are being dug for a new sewer line in
Luv Kush Colony, in Sawai Madhopur, Rajasthan.
There is a plan to offer an internship program for
500 female engineering students during phase 4.

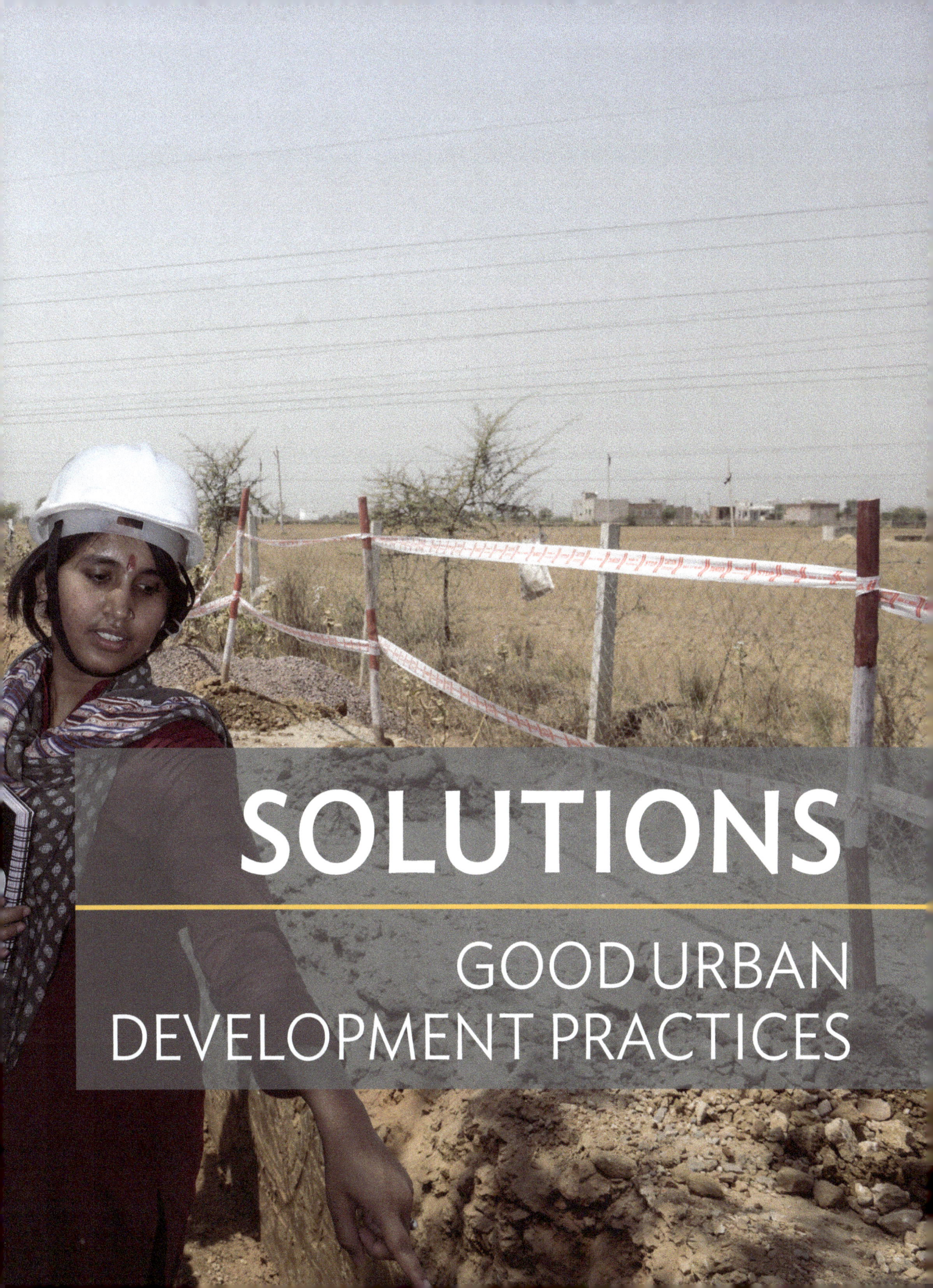

SOLUTIONS

GOOD URBAN DEVELOPMENT PRACTICES

What distinguishes RUIDP as a project management entity has been its ability to incorporate lessons into its daily and systematic practices over a long operational period. This continuous institutional strengthening has fostered a corporate culture that treats efficiency and quality as a double bottom line. The ADB–RUIDP partnership exemplifies the key principles and practices that ADB encourages its operational staff to adhere to when designing investments for more livable cities (and which this chapter explores): investing in strategic zones and corridors rather than widely across a country; taking the long view of development; building long-term investment partnerships with government clients; involving the public in urban planning and investment design; and transforming cities with a critical mass of financing and capacity building, rather than just making modest improvements within a single sector of a single city.

The solutions, lessons, and experiences that RUIDP has garnered are presented in this chapter as good practices for other municipalities to follow. The guidelines cover the stages of the project management cycle: selection and design, preparation and implementation, and monitoring and evaluation. Many of the good practices are based on capacity building and lessons learned that were incorporated into the design and implementation of subsequent investment phases. The guidance provided in the section below on preparation and implementation stage is organized according to the standard aspects of project management: organizational arrangements and principles, financial management, procurement, and implementation.

Project Selection and Design

Rather than spreading resources thinly across several cities in this vast country, ADB focused comprehensive resources on cities within a single state, Rajasthan, to develop a viable model for replicable urban development. RUIDP program cities were selected strategically in a phased order of priority, according to their potential to contribute to the state's overall economic growth, while maintaining geographic balance.

Economists had forecasted high economic growth in the state. As an example of the predicted growth, almost 40% of the length of dedicated freight transported via the Delhi–Mumbai Industrial Corridor would be passing through Rajasthan (58% of Rajasthan is within the corridor's influence area). For the anticipated high growth to translate into quality growth, however, cities throughout the state would need infrastructure capable of absorbing urban migration. Currently, 25% of the state's population lives in cities where there is a 3% annual growth rate. By 2026, nearly 30% of the state's population is expected to be living in urban areas.

Group Project Cities by Type, Phase

The RUIDP investments are being spread among cities across the state and in four phases (Figure 3). Investments flowed first to the state's most populous cities, with the major urban economies, and then to medium-sized and small cities and towns, as follows:

- Phase 1 began with the state's six largest cities (all divisional headquarters), with a combined population of 7 million.
- Phase 2 focused on 15 cities of varying sizes.
- Phase 3, still being implemented as of early 2021, is focusing on six cities (all district headquarters) with populations of 100,000 or more.

- Phase 4 began implementation in late 2020 for secondary towns with populations of 50,000 to 100,000, and for small heritage cities of about 20,000 population (with ADB supporting 14 towns initially, and possibly additional towns identified later for future investments).

ADB and the state government use two basic criteria when mapping the geographic focal areas of the project: the amount of secured financing and the capacity of the prospective cities to implement and monitor projects. When choosing investments, the approach is to focus on components that can be accomplished within the project's financial means, rather than spreading investments too thinly or assuming unsecured financing from other partners. Assessing and building local capacity has also been key to RUIDP's ability to complete projects while adhering to quality standards, budgets, and schedules.

Figure 3: Map of the Rajasthan Urban Infrastructure Development Project

Source: Asian Development Bank.

Create Clear Site Selection Factors

To determine the cities to be selected for the project, the state government decision makers were guided by a needs assessment that looked closely at the growth potential of every prospective project city.[14] Initially, the investment program began with the state's most economically important growth engines that also had the highest investment capacity. As RUIDP improved its management skills and project implementation capacity, the investment program turned its attention to smaller cities, where higher social impact was ensured, although the potential for economic returns may be lower. The selection of sites for each phase of RUIDP has been influenced by different factors:

City selection for phase 1. Prior to phase 1 of RUIDP, there had been no huge investments in Rajasthan's urban sector, so the municipal services in the towns were poor. Considering this, under phase I, ADB and the state government chose six major cities: Ajmer, Bikaner, Jaipur, Jodhpur, Kota, and Udaipur. The selected cities were the administrative, industrial, and commercial nerve centers of the state, besides being important tourist centers. They were also of significant cultural, economic, and historical value.

Town selection for phase 2. The town selection process for phase 2 took other national urban development investments into account. The Indian government launched the Jawaharlal Nehru National Urban Renewal Mission and the Urban Infrastructure Development Scheme for Small and Medium Towns in 2005. RUIDP phase 2 considered the scope of these national government schemes when selecting its own 15 towns, which were large in size, the administrative headquarters of their districts, and geographically spread across the state.

Town selection for phase 3. In 2015, the Indian government launched the Atal Mission for Rejuvenation and Urban Transformation (AMRUT) and the Smart Cities Mission, both focused on improving the water supply, sewerage facilities, septage management, drainage, nonmotorized transport, and green infrastructure in 29 towns with populations over 100,000. In line with AMRUT, the project loan component of RUIDP phase 3 has included the remaining six district headquarters of the state. Program loan funds were also being used to improve the infrastructure facilities in another seven towns in Rajasthan.

Town selection for phase 4. The state government developed a water supply investment road map in 2014 that sought to address the short-term and long-term needs of small towns. In these towns, which have not yet received ADB support, water supply coverage could be relatively high, but the water quality is poor and service is intermittent. For RUIDP's phase 4, the state government has selected 32 towns with populations of 20,000 to 100,000 that had not been covered by any of the national schemes, plus another 10 towns that have historical significance and heritage value. Of those, ADB has identified 14 towns for urgent investment, and is considering further support in subsequent phases.

---

[14] As a standard process, prior to a loan agreement with the state government, ADB finances a project preparatory technical assistance (PPTA), whereby consultants conduct a detailed needs assessment of the towns and sectors. The PPTA generates detailed project designs that are economically, financially, and technically feasible. This ensures economic and social returns on any investments, as well as the capacity to manage and sustain the investments.

Spread the Impact across Urban Sectors

The fundamental component of RUIDP in any project city has been the water supply, but a critical mass of infrastructure and capacity development have also been needed to transform Rajasthan's cities. At the beginning, the infrastructure and capacity baselines for most cities were so limited that improving just the water supply system and services alone would not have improved the long-term economic prospects of these cities.

Phase 1 of RUIDP had the most ambitious scope of works, which included urban heritage rehabilitation; hospitals; fire stations; and slum redevelopment; as well as the typical multisector urban programs, usually a mix of works focused on water supply, sanitation, drainage, solid waste management, and roads. Not every sector experienced a major impact from the project, but government officials said that some works (such as heritage restoration and hospital renovations) built tremendous public goodwill toward RUIDP.

Over time, RUIDP has narrowed its scope to sectors related to water, with a greater emphasis on institutional development. Phase 3 focuses more on water supply, sanitation, and drainage, but with greater coverage rates. During the previous phases, the investments only covered parts of project cities, and accounted for only a share of increased water availability. Because Rajasthan is not endowed with water resources, phases 1 and 2 merely augmented supplies, increasing their availability from 1–2 hours every 2–3 days to 1–2 hours daily—a 300% increase in water availability in a desert state. Phase 3 aims to achieve water supplies 24 hours a day, 7 days a week (24/7) and 100% coverage of the project cities. This has required completely new systems. Phase 3 has also introduced reforms, policies, and capacity-building programs for urban local bodies (ULBs). Phase 4 will also pursue 24/7 water supplies and appropriate sewerage and drainage systems for small towns. During all the phases, slum areas were and will continue to be among the first areas to be connected.

The multisector design of the investments evolved from consultations. The same questions were asked of everyone: What are the greatest needs, and where are they found? The single most common development issue facing any city, town, or hamlet anywhere in Rajasthan was water. There is either not enough of it (most of the time) or too much of it (during the monsoons). Sanitation and drainage were the two most common subsidiary water problems that affected urban environments, threatening people's health, safety, and wallets, especially during the monsoon season, when urban commerce and many ground-level stores and homes were inundated by mucky floodwaters.

Invest in a Long-Term Partnership

ADB and the state government understood from the beginning that developing Rajasthan's cities into competitive, equitable, and environmentally livable places would not be a sprint across an 8-year project timeline. Urban development in Rajasthan would take decades. ADB and the state government charted a strategic course; built new training grounds; put only the best professionals in the race; and called for new rules, regulations, and systems that would be implemented over time, as capacity developed.

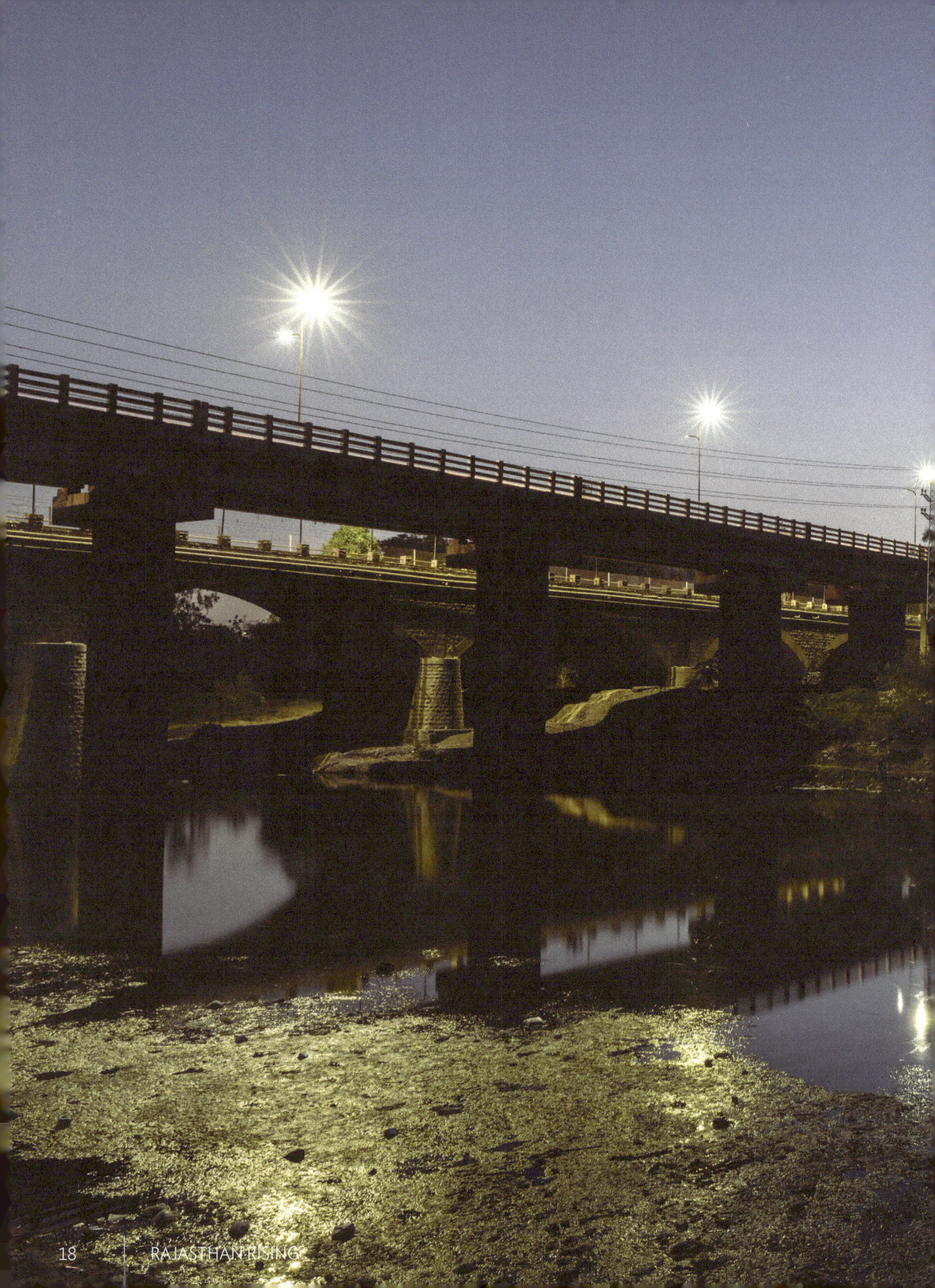

Making a way. ADB's investments in RUIDP supported the construction of road-bridges over waterways and railroads, improving accessibility within cities and easing traffic congestion. The ADB-financed road-bridge pictured here is over the Berach river in Chittorgarh, Rajasthan.

Emphasize Public Sector Management

The financial sustainability of projects is routinely threatened by weak public management systems. Livable cities require revenues for operation and maintenance (O&M). Historically, ULBs have been reluctant to raise tariffs or to reform their tax systems. This has been evident in low O&M expenditures, low tariff collection rates, institutional inefficiency, lack of corporate good practices, and high nonrevenue water levels and other service delivery constraints.

The first two phases of investments in Rajasthan included a standard program for developing the implementing agencies' staff, capacity, and systems for project management, procurement, financial controls, safeguards, and monitoring for the intended benefits (Impact Story 2). By the third phase, with nearly 15 years of experience in many sectors, ADB and the state government embarked on reforms. A $250 million program loan provided the state government with the resources to study its options for managing cities; sustaining infrastructure; and finding other sources of capital for urban development, particularly for O&M expenses. The reform program addressed three areas of public sector management: institutional strengthening, improvements in urban governance, and capacity building.

The third chapter of this report, "Results: Livable Cities," details the RUIDP policy objectives and how the project has achieved them. Individually and collectively, the policy objectives have created an enabling environment for more effective public sector management and the development of more livable cities.

Do Not Assume Consensus, Build It

As desperate as cities are for infrastructure, RUIDP learned in phase 1 that it can be difficult to convince ULBs that infrastructure is worth taking out a loan for. At the beginning, RUIDP was too new to have the solid reputation it has today. It was a freshly established group, hardly the formidable, unrivaled institution it has since become. Big urban development programs were new to India. The central government's national programs and missions had not yet pivoted from rural to urban development, though that was to happen shortly. Moreover, for ADB, Rajasthan was new investment territory. ADB already had (and continues to have) successful urban investments in Karnataka, but the Rajasthan investment was then only starting to shape up to be its largest urban sector loan.

There was a lot at stake, and everyone on the ground was aware of that. Most of the project cities were getting by on only an hour of water supply every couple of days, but tampering with that precious hour was nerve-wracking. The development of major urban infrastructure in poorly outfitted places can take up to a decade to complete, once all of the capacity gaps, complications in procurement, and contractor delays are considered. For elected officials, their stars rise and fall on many things, and a botched or belabored water project would be a big risk. As ADB acknowledges in its urban operations strategy, "Political term limits are often at odds with long-term development."

For Big Infrastructure, Use Client's Baseline to Determine Financing, Capacity-Building Needs

The Rajasthan Urban Infrastructure Development Project (RUIDP) experienced the usual delays—having to find a building with enough space, recruit staff, engage consultants, and manage common political pressures. RUIDP was a new institution, but it was still part of the established system. The program hobbled along for a few years, not gaining any real traction. The initial setbacks were not due to a lack of good leadership, but to a lack of experience with such major international development financing. This was also first investment in Rajasthan by the Asian Development Bank (ADB).

"No one knew how to do this project," said Ashok Srivastava, who was one of the earliest staff members of RUIDP before joining ADB, where he is now a senior urban project officer. "They didn't know how this could be done. It was a new project, new institution. It was not just some department of engineers." Slow starts like this are common, and costly.

The Rajasthan experience taught ADB's South Asia urban operations staff to do business differently. Start-ups with new government clients might not have the required capacity development. With more simple infrastructure projects, governments could learn how to procure consultants, contractors, goods, and equipment that are up to ADB standards—although this would involve the time-consuming process of trial and error. For example, ADB's South Asia Urban Division has said that it would not likely lend a new government client $300 million at first, but it would lend $70 million–$80 million, to get the capacity building started.

Progress on institutional development can be slow because capacity building happens by walking a government department or project office through the day-to-day process of doing everything more sustainably. Government clients must adopt ADB's policies and practices with regard to social safeguards, procurement procedures, financial management, and auditing.

Government contractors must also adopt ADB's stringent procurement procedures and social safeguard policies. Indeed, the contractors that have done business with RUIDP have come to expect these policies and standards from other government clients, and they go on to win major national tenders because of their experience with ADB and RUIDP.

"What you do in the beginning is the most important," said G.S. Hada, RUIDP additional project director, in 2018. He has worked for RUIDP intermittently since 2005. "Others will follow—the departments, the agencies—but you have to do the hard work first."

RUIDP has adopted higher standards for the entire project cycle, and boasts of ever-improving detailed designs, procurement packages, higher-quality bids, and innovations.

> ## ❝ PROJECT VOICES
>
> **What you do in the beginning is the most important. Others will follow— the departments, the agencies—but you have to do the hard work first.**
>
> G.S. Hada, RUIDP additional project director

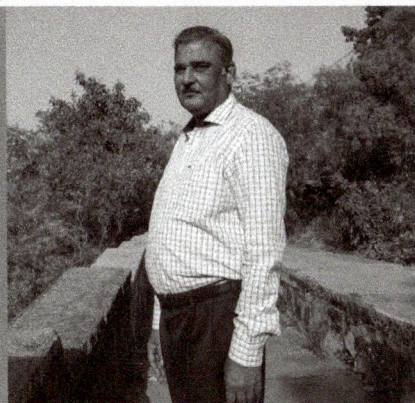

Source: Authors.

Water supply and sanitation are essential to cities and public health and the poor, but they aren't enough, not enough to make the city livable for the poor.

Preetam Yashvant, medical doctor and former RUIDP project director and current commissioner for Rajasthan's Commercial Taxes Department

Former RUIDP Project Director Preetam Yashvant (currently the commissioner for Rajasthan's Commercial Taxes Department) spoke most fervently about the program's investments, which he felt had less to do with water and everything to do with what makes the poor feel more secure in urban areas: "Water supply and sanitation are essential to cities and public health and the poor, but they aren't enough, not enough to make the city livable for the poor."

RUIDP's fervent approach to public consultations and its mainstreaming of communications, awareness, and public participation into its engineering operations have helped build consensus in favor of the projects. Impact Story 3 provides an illustrative lesson in the importance of project communications.

Give Everyone a Voice in Project Selection

In the initial phase of determining the scope of works in a proposed city, RUIDP organizes a presentation and discussion forum with the concerned local body, chairman and councillors, the district collector, the commissioner, and the municipal engineering staff. In this setting, RUIDP outlines the major objectives of the investment program, the funds available, and the proposed interventions. A similar meeting is held later to present the draft of the detailed project design.

Each stakeholder group has its unique perspectives and values, which have helped designers to create city investments that are more relevant, in demand, and transformative. The government stakeholders are essential for identifying the hurdles and roadblocks that could arise with a particular proposed project, clearances required, and local policies. Public representatives and citizens are key to generating public awareness; understanding the citizen's perception of needs and expectations; and to identifying opportunities for their participation in the design, implementation, and monitoring of projects.

Confusion, Delays in Chittorgarh Teach a Lesson in Communicating Early and Often

During phase 2 of the Rajasthan Urban Infrastructure Development Project (RUIDP), plans to construct sewage treatment plants met with delays and public opposition, which are common, but preventable. Residents in the vicinity of proposed plants often worry about odors, soil and water contamination, and the related construction traffic. RUIDP's experience in the city of Chittorgarh taught a valuable lesson in the importance of communicating early and often to avoid project delays.

Chittorgarh had no sewerage system, and the RUIDP investment called for a 5 million-liter-per-day treatment plant on municipal land at the edge of a semi urban hamlet, Boie Khera. To access the site of the plant, the construction crews needed to pass through Boie Khera.

The hamlet is a collection of concrete huts and stone-stacked walls. The residents are farmers and occasional day laborers. Trouble started when the contractor began building the perimeter wall. RUIDP had followed its communication and consultation protocols in identifying the projects and subprojects, but the residents of Boie Khera were confused. The said that they had begun asking local officials what was going on. RUIDP hosted a community meeting to explain the project, but by then the residents were distrustful. Misinformation had begun spreading.

RUIDP hosted a visit for village residents to another site, where there was a plant already in operation, to prove that there would be no odor or sludge discharge. RUIDP engineers noted that the residents were pleasantly surprised and began to support the project, but the larger community wanted to leverage the project for local improvements. So, roads were blocked, legal injunctions were filed, and the work was delayed for 2.5 years. The courts ruled in favor of the project, and the plant was eventually built.

"In phase 1 investments, there was no resistance like in Chittorgarh, because they were bigger cities. There [were] already some sewerage systems, so the idea wasn't new," said Babulal Sharma, team leader and communication expert for RUIDP's Community Awareness and Participation Program. Chittorgarh was the location of the second sewage treatment plant to be built during phase 2. The first plant, in the city of Sawai Madhopur, was not near any settlement, so the engineers and contractors did not experience the kind of resistance they did in Chittorgarh.

RUIDP increased its communication efforts before the construction of other sewage treatment plants. Phase 2 saw the completion of 13 such plants, in towns similar to Chittorgarh. There was opposition, but never as detrimental as that faced in Boie Khera.

"There could have been earlier communication," said a member of RUIDP's communications team. "The delays could have been avoided. But we learned."

Source: Authors.

Former RUIDP Project Director Jitendra Kumar Soni said, "RUIDP valued 'people-centered' developed early on. It understood that people were not just the beneficiaries, but also the customers. People pay taxes and tariffs, and they deserve to be satisfied [with] the services they are paying for and with the government representing their needs."

In this way, RUIDP can respond to the groundswell of local needs, demands, and wishes (Impact Story 4).

Roads over Railways Ease Traffic and Boost Growth and Connectivity

Consultations with stakeholders in the Rajasthan Urban Infrastructure Development Project (RUIDP) revealed that roads over railways were in high demand because they could ease the heavy traffic in Rajasthan's cities. They are critically needed infrastructure that can boost economic growth, connectivity, and efficiency in cities. Jodhpur was one of the project cities that clamored for these roads as a means of improving its transport system.

"Everyone thought all of the crossings should be included," said Ravi Suthar, an environmental consultant with RUIDP. "You take the suggestions and preferences of all the line agencies, but then you have to go to the sites because everything can change on the site visits. There are ideas that are just not possible because of the area or the budget. So, we chose the most critical crossings to build rail over bridges."

The Asian Development Bank financed four of the five needed roads over railroads in high-traffic areas in Jodhpur: near a hub of agricultural and engineering colleges, at a vegetable market, in an industrial zone, and over the national highway to the town of Jaisalmer.

Railway crossings are traffic bottlenecks in cities across Rajasthan, so RUIDP has constructed key roads over railroad tracks for pedestrians and vehicles. Ravi Suthar, an environmental engineer and longtime consultant with RUIDP supervised many projects like this rail over bridge in the busy city of Jodhpur, Rajasthan, India.

Source: Authors.

The lists representing the input from the various stakeholders make their rounds through the bureaucracy, vetted along the way by engineers, economists, administrators, and elected officials. The different perceptions of the various levels of government and of the public are then brought into alignment in a process that refines and prioritizes subprojects to create a package attractive enough for the municipalities.

Public consultations have proven to be a very practical way for RUIDP to prepare for slum development work and empower local women in the process. Through these consultations, women have found opportunities to influence the design of slum improvements, express their interest in skills training, mobilize the community to ensure a smooth implementation, and promote a higher awareness among the residents of what will be expected of them as paying customers of water and wastewater services. Involving the community from the design to the monitoring stage is a customer-focused approach that gives the public more confidence in the utility services.

Preparation and Implementation

Organizational Arrangement and Principles

To lead and manage a new kind of work culture, ADB envisioned something more ambitious than any prior state program or ADB urban operation in the country. The standard practice of establishing a project management office within an existing government office would have set the project up for failure. Sekhar Bonu, former director of ADB's South Asia Urban and Water Division, explained why a different approach was and still is needed for project design, implementation, and management: "Sometimes you may have an institution or office with really creative individuals, who together would make a great team. But then they have no power. Everything they want to do or want to try has to go through layers of bureaucratic approvals. It's disheartening and disempowering to them."

ADB and the state government decided to establish an autonomous, sustainable corporation that would oversee urban development projects and programs in Rajasthan. In a move that was a bit shortsighted, the institution was given the name of the first phase of the ADB investment initiative, the Rajasthan Urban Infrastructure Development Project (RUIDP), but it has since outgrown that name, having evolved into a well-known project for overall urban development, not just infrastructure. RUIDP was established in 1999 under the state's Urban Development Department (now within the Local Self Government Department). It has the advantage of autonomy, with independent funding sources (though mostly still from ADB) and the freedom to hire staff, organize itself, handle procurement, and manage its project investments. As in any typical project office, RUIDP's core staff (not consultants, contractors, etc.) are seconded from relevant government departments and agencies, but the difference is that RUIDP's recruits are subject to a stringent vetting process to ensure that only those with the greatest technical or managerial experience or potential are accepted; there are no political appointments, and no one is recruited based on seniority. RUIDP staff are often retained for long tenures (sometimes more than a decade), and they answer only to RUIDP, with no responsibility to their original departments or agencies. Moreover, RUIDP is exempt from most standard government procedures, so it is freer to adopt international good practices. All day-to-day financial, management, and technical decisions are the responsibility of the project director, and are generally not subject to external government protocols.

RUIDP's hallmark is its efficient design and execution of diverse urban projects. Over its 20 years of operations, it has become an experienced organization specialized in project management and implementation, with a portfolio that has expanded beyond ADB to include state and national development programs. A multistakeholder organizational structure provides the oversight.

In 2016, RUIDP combined with a state-owned urban housing company and an urban finance corporation to form a state-level entity—the Rajasthan Urban Drinking Water, Sewerage & Infrastructure Corporation (RUDSICO)—which was responsible for implementing urban schemes funded by the state and national governments.[15] RUDSICO is now assisting with state and national programs as well as additional mega-projects related to water supply, sanitation, housing, roads, and other urban infrastructure. Rather than relying on a centralized project management structure, RUDSICO depends on local organizations that have sufficient financial and administrative autonomy to take on project implementation duties.

A corporation dedicated to urban development investments is capable of quick decision-making, faster disbursement of funds, and a clear allocation of roles and responsibilities—all of which is a hedge against interference and delays caused by unrelated government tasks. RUDSICO staff need not divide their time between their project responsibilities and the non-project expectations of some government agency.

Require Elite Leadership on a Full-Time Basis

An often-cited success factor of RUIDP is its leadership and staff. RUIDP is led by a dedicated project director from the elite Indian Administrative Service (IAS). Mounted on the wall behind the desk and chair of the RUIDP project director is a large wooden plaque inscribed with the names of every project director for RUIDP—a succession of 15 of them since 2000. The short tenures were the tradeoff for having elite bureaucrats serve in the post, as their tenure is typically 2 years in any position.

---

15   The other two components that merged to form RUDSICO were Rajasthan Avas Vikas and Infrastructure Limited, a company founded to address urban housing issues in the state, and the Rajasthan Urban Infrastructure Finance & Development Corporation Limited, an urban finance company that implemented projects funded by the state and national governments.

As a "special project vehicle" institution, RUIDP does not have its own staff, but instead relies on staff deputed from various state government departments and agencies. Consisting of engineers and other support personnel, the staff comes mainly from the Public Health Engineering Department (PHED), ULBs, the Town Planning Department, the Urban Development and Housing Department, the Public Works Department, and the Department of Finance. Project implementation units exist in each project city and town, and are assisted by design, supervision, and project management consultants. City-level committees monitor the progress of the construction of infrastructure, which RUIDP turns over to the participating cities and towns upon completion. RUIDP is responsible for ensuring that the ULBs and the government departments are trained for the operation and maintenance (O&M) of the assets. RUIDP's performance has been weak with regard to O&M, but recent investment phases have allocated more resources to capacity building in this area.

Starting in the early, formative years of RUIDP, project directors have carefully supervised the functions and responsibilities of the organization. The discipline enforced by these IAS officers has resulted in an institutional culture resembling that of a modern corporation, which is typically characterized by a strong work ethic. Indeed, staff members have described 12-hour days that pass without noticing the clock, with leisurely lunches a foregone custom because of critical deadlines. Some project directors have been known for arriving first and leaving last, often working 15-hour days (Impact Story 6).

Hire Only the Best, Brightest Technical Staff, on a Full-Time Basis

When it comes to recruitment, RUIDP prioritizes work ethic over specialization, seniority, and especially academic or political pedigree.

"We were looking for the right work ethic, not specialization," said Ashok Srivastava, who was an early RUIDP staff member before joining ADB, where he is now a senior urban project officer at the India Resident Mission. "It took time identifying the best fits. There were very good engineers who just wanted to do a very good job and come to a new, clean, transparent organization." A colleague of his at ADB, Pushkar Srivastava, also a senior urban project officer at the resident mission, said, "You need a critical mass of good people to handle this size of investment. RUIDP had strength in numbers and strength in skill."

RUIDP has gathered and replenished its staff with junior, mid-level, and senior professionals, creating a leadership pipeline through which professionals can advance their careers within the institution. Former RUIDP Project Director Naveen Mahajan (now the secretary of Rajasthan's Water Resources Department) said that "the backbone of RUIDP is its great team of engineers, who were selected by a rigorous screening mechanism, resulting in a better set of human and technical manpower." Kush Kumar, a junior engineer at one of RUIDP's project offices, remembers when he was hired in 2015. "I had heard that if RUIDP is doing the work, it will be done. So, I was excited when I got this job," he said. "I am just starting my career, but here I get a chance to work on major projects."

Planning for the succession of senior staff is critical for sustaining RUIDP's success. Neeta Pokhrel, currently unit head of project administration for ADB's South Asia Urban and Water Division, has worked with RUIDP since 2007, and knows the staff and operations well. "Some of the staff have been with RUIDP for a long time, and have been instrumental in retaining the institutional memory in RUIDP on best practices and lessons learnt on project delivery, and also in training the new generation of staff there," she said.

Competency and Agility of Project Tested over 8 Days

The seasonal release of irrigation water is not something to be jeopardized, ever. Yet that is exactly what the Rajasthan Urban Infrastructure Development Project (RUIDP) needed to do to finish laying a critical portion of a sewerage pipeline on the eastern border town of Bharatpur. It had to excavate 6 meters below the canal in order to continue laying a 2-kilometer pipeline. The pipeline was 1.6 meters in diameter.

The Government of Rajasthan would not allow RUIDP to work beneath the canal during flow season. If RUIDP wanted to lay the pipe, it had to finish before the first seasonal release, due in 8 days. It was the ultimate test of RUIDP's technical ability.

RUIDP management sent executive engineer Krishna Kumar Agarwal to complete the job. Missing that 8-day window would mean a 6-month delay in the project.

"Releasing that irrigation is a very sensitive issue. And it is also very political," Agarwal explained. The irrigation water would serve farmers in Rajasthan, but also a neighboring state to the east, Uttar Pradesh. Delaying the release of irrigation water would have quickly become a political and economic issue at the highest level between the two states.

"I put my chair on that site and didn't ever leave," Agarwal said. "I slept there. I ate there. The district collector [the CEO for the district] came twice to check on me and called continuously because, if that work did not finish in time, I could expect Rajasthan's chief minister to be on-site. The release of the irrigation water is that sensitive."

He devised a 24-hour work plan with a 100-strong workforce. And he employed horizontal directional drilling, a method of trenchless excavation, for the critical portions, and open excavation for the rest. The canal side walls and floor, a total 30 meters in length, were concrete lined to avoid the possibility of water infiltration.

Agarwal finished the work 2 days early.

Just 8 days before the state of Rajasthan's much anticipated seasonal release of irrigation water to farmers, RUIDP needed to lay a critical pipeline underneath the canal to avoid costly and lengthy project delays. RUIDP executive engineer Krishna Kumar Agarwal was in charge of the 24/7 operation. He finished the work 2 days ahead of schedule.

Source: Authors.

A Development Ecosystem with a Critical Mass of Competence

The trifecta of having the right professionals, systems, and practices has created what some staff at the Asian Development Bank (ADB) call a "development ecosystem" within the Rajasthan Urban Infrastructure Development Project (RUIDP). It is what every municipality requires: a critical mass of competent financiers, administrators, bureaucrats, engineers, and consultants who are highly disciplined and follow well-designed systems and procedures.

Sangay Penjor, director of ADB's East Asia Urban and Social Sectors Division, experienced this synergy and efficiency when he led ADB's Rajasthan operations team during phase 2 of RUIDP. He talked about the difference this made for project missions. "It was not just one person we would work with in Rajasthan, but a whole team," he explained. "Typically, on some projects elsewhere, we—the ADB delegation—may just be sitting with just one person, the head or deputy. That person may be very good and efficient, but any time we had questions, he or she would have to call someone. Resources were very ad hoc. We would have to sometimes wait 2 or 3 days for someone to get back to us on a question. What happens is we lose our focus. But when I compare the meetings I would have in Rajasthan to those elsewhere, they were much more meaningful and thorough discussions. There would be the head, but also a long table of specialists, and we sat together figuring things out. Meetings were long and detailed because we could ask all our questions right there."

One ADB manager who was present through much of RUIDP's life cycle thus far attributed this development ecosystem to the quality of the program's leaders and rank and file. "Institutions are the engines of capacity and efficiency. These are sometimes very rhetorical words, but there is truth to them, too," he said. "It's more a matter of how you develop institutions that we should focus on."

Source: Authors.

"But the institutional memory and capacity to train younger generation will leave as the very experienced and knowledgeable staff retire or move on to other work, and that is already happening. Sufficient and timely succession planning needs to be tackled soon for the new generation of staff that will eventually take over" (Impact Story 7).

Let Needs and Lessons Learned Determine Use of Consultants, Instead of Standard Practice

RUIDP has accumulated vast experience in managing consultants over a period of 20 years, and has changed the way it works with consultants based on the lessons learned during the project phases. Owing to RUIDP's lack of technical capacity during phase 1, international experts were appointed as project management consultants (PMCs). Guided by ADB and the PMCs, RUIDP improved its internal capacities during phase 1, and it appointed national consultants for phase 2: one PMC and three design supervision consultants (DSCs). RUIDP experienced the constraints of having two different sets of consultants (PMC and DSCs). The main constraints included a lack of coordination and sharing of responsibility between the PMC and DSCs, causing several delays and hindering the completion of projects. In phase 3, RUIDP combined the PMC and DSC roles, appointing consultants who specialized in both project management and design supervision, and who were wholly responsible for both the design and implementation of the works. Because phase 3 includes specialized projects such as distribution systems in district metered areas (DMAs) and 24/7 water supplies, international consultants were selected for this combined role.

Highly Competent Professionals Foster Competition, but Systems Also Help

The cadre of engineers, consultants, and contractors who were groomed by the Rajasthan Urban Infrastructure Development Project (RUIDP) have become exemplary sector experts, and have either made their careers with RUIDP or have repositioned themselves as national or international consultants with government and development organizations.

Staff members at the Asian Development Bank (ADB) who are familiar with RUIDP's operations estimate that Rajasthan has produced 20% to 30% of ADB's consultants in the country.

While this helps to spread best practices and develop capacity, the turnover rate could have been disruptive to RUIDP operations, if it were not for the emphasis on investment in systems.

ADB operations staff members have explained how their emphasis on institution building was an attempt to achieve sustainability. "The institution is the brain. It has the ability to turn ideas into action," said Sekhar Bonu, a former director of ADB's urban operations in India, when interviewed for this report. "And we haven't figured out this magic for every place ADB is working because it's all tacit and there is a lot of movement of people. Creating a legacy like we are doing in Rajasthan is difficult. Knowledge is gone when people leave. But if you create a bureaucracy with new systems and new norms, it is more permanent and can survive individuals."

Ravi Suthar, who joined RUIDP as a fresh engineering graduate in 2005, said that he had turned down other job offers. He now feels too invested in RUIDP to leave, having learned the entire project cycle. When he started, RUIDP was nearing the end of phase 1. He has supervised many projects since then, so he is now involved in the preparation of detailed project reports for towns selected for phase 4.

"I like working for externally funded projects because they are more complex. Real challenges are there," he said. "In RUIDP, I'm the engineer and I get to do the work. I can suggest improvements. It's very progressive. For example, if the contractor has an issue, we are here to look after design and quality. I have the courage to stand up to the contractor. In a government department, I would have constraints [on speaking up]. The client does not want a 'yes man.' RUIDP operates like an independent corporation."

Source: Authors.

In phase 4, RUIDP and ULBs will hire consultants to prepare the detailed project reports before the actual signing of the loan. This will help RUIDP utilize the entire loan period for project implementation. As the project towns in RUIDP phase 4 will be smaller, there will be a need to improve the capacities of the ULBs. For this reason, capacity building and institutional strengthening have been added to the responsibilities of the PMCs, so they will be referred to as "project-management and capacity-building consultants." The number of towns participating in phase 4 will be large, so two DSCs are being appointed, one to assist the project implementation units (PIUs) in the project cities and towns, and the other to assist the project management unit (PMU), which is headquartered in Jaipur.

Manage Both the Program and Project Levels

RUIDP operates at both the program and project levels, demonstrating strong leadership, complex stakeholder coordination, technical expertise, implementation prowess, and professional managerial skills (Impact Story 7). The program cycle involves facilitating broad stakeholder consensus on the scope of investments, beginning the process with local-level stakeholders, and continuing up the decision-making ladder to the state level. RUIDP has been instrumental in securing funding for major urban initiatives, remaining accountable to financiers such as the central government and ADB, and it has become adept at complex procurement, project management, monitoring, and evaluation processes. The valuable lessons learned during RUIDP implementation may be replicated across states in India because of the many common elements in the country's urban institutional landscapes.

"RUIDP staff are assertive, know their client and market, and over the years of delivering projects, have learned to foresee and manage risks quite well," said Neeta Pokhrel, unit head for project administration in ADB's South Asia Urban and Water Division. "They have earned their respect, both internally and externally, as experts in what they are doing, and thus have become quite resilient and effective in delivering their projects. They are now setting examples and benchmarks for similar entities in India. In our ADB-supported projects, we are also sending some of our counterparts from other states to cross-learn from them."

" PROJECT VOICES

RUIDP staff are assertive, know their client and market, and over the years of delivering projects, have learned to foresee and manage risks quite well. … In our ADB-supported projects, we are also sending some of our counterparts from other states to cross-learn from them.

Neeta Pokhrel, unit head for project administration in ADB's South Asia
Urban and Water Division

RUIDP also functions as a statewide entity, in addition to its role in city-level project management. At the program (i.e., state) level, it encompasses a constellation of cities, simultaneously implementing multisector urban development packages that deliver. RUIDP operates as a PMU, and is headquartered in Jaipur, with a network of PIUs in the cities where its urban development projects are being implemented. The city-based PIUs facilitate and supervise the design, implementation, and monitoring of local works. A flexible approach to staff mobility between the state headquarters and the PIUs has been one of the secrets of RUIDP's success.

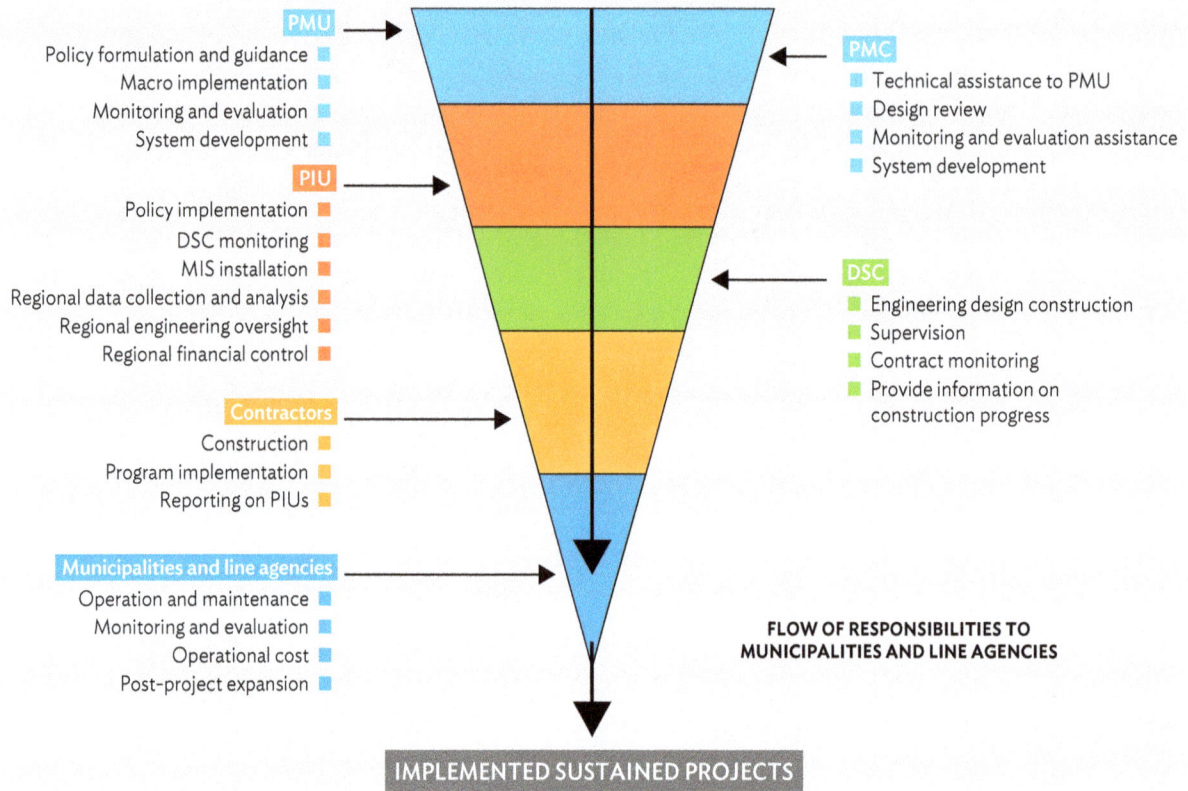

Figure 4: Organizational Setup for Project Management

PMU
- Policy formulation and guidance
- Macro implementation
- Monitoring and evaluation
- System development

PIU
- Policy implementation
- DSC monitoring
- MIS installation
- Regional data collection and analysis
- Regional engineering oversight
- Regional financial control

Contractors
- Construction
- Program implementation
- Reporting on PIUs

Municipalities and line agencies
- Operation and maintenance
- Monitoring and evaluation
- Operational cost
- Post-project expansion

PMC
- Technical assistance to PMU
- Design review
- Monitoring and evaluation assistance
- System development

DSC
- Engineering design construction
- Supervision
- Contract monitoring
- Provide information on construction progress

FLOW OF RESPONSIBILITIES TO MUNICIPALITIES AND LINE AGENCIES

IMPLEMENTED SUSTAINED PROJECTS

DSC = design supervision consultant, MIS = management information system, PIU = project implementation unit, PMC = project management consultant, PMU = project management unit.

Source: Rajasthan Urban Infrastructure Development Project.

The PMU and the PIUs in the participating towns and cities need both DSCs and the PMCs for support. Figure 4 illustrates the arrangement of key organizations and their roles and responsibilities in the program or project cycle.

Project management unit. Based in Jaipur, the PMU directs, coordinates, and manages all program activities, including project design, implementation, budgeting and financial planning, benefit monitoring and evaluation, institutional and policy development, promotion of community participation, and coordination of the work of all the consulting services. Having an IAS officer as the project director is considered advantageous for an effective coordination with the other state departments and with the national government. The PMU has a strong technical team with expertise in water and sewerage project implementation, led by two chief engineers. It also has financial and accountancy staff, headed by a financial advisor and deputed Department of Finance staff, who help with the coordination between RUIDP and the finance department.

Project implementation units. Unlike the PMU, based in Jaipur, the PIUs operate in the project towns and cities like typical temporary project management offices, though the engineering staff can be transferred by RUIDP between PIUs, enabling the sharing of capacity and knowledge throughout the program over time.

The PIUs are responsible for planning and implementing all of the project components in the project-designated towns and cities. They also ensure that the project activities are carried out within the estimated costs and that they adhere to acceptable quality standards. A PIU is established in a project-designated town or city immediately after the award of an RUIDP contract to the contractor.

The PIU is headed by either a superintendent engineer or an executive engineer, depending on the size of the investment in the town or city. For example, in phases 1 and 3, each PIU has been headed by a superintendent engineer, typically an officer with more than 20 years of field experience, as the investments during these phases have been substantial. Additional engineers and administrative staff support the PIU head. The PIUs are closed after the completion of a project, and the PIU staff are then either transferred to other PIUs or sent back to their original departments. The PIUs are supported by DSCs in each town or city to provide additional managerial and technical support.

Project management consultants and design supervision consultants. ADB and RUIDP believe that the success of the program is also attributable to its strong consultants, particularly the PMCs and the DSCs.

PMCs assist RUIDP in carrying out project responsibilities and the implementation of decisions. The major responsibilities of the PMC are
- securing the selection and approval of project components,
- analyzing and securing the approval of conceptual and final designs and estimates for all infrastructure projects in each project city,
- assisting the PMU in issuing all tender documents pertaining to the construction of infrastructure projects,
- assisting the PMU in evaluating and selecting all contractors responsible for the construction of selected aspects of the infrastructure subprojects built under the aegis of RUIDP, and
- overseeing the activities of the DSCs located in the project cities.

DSCs provide support to multiple institutional stakeholders: the PMU, PIUs, ULBs, and municipal line agencies for the efficient preparation and implementation of subprojects. Each consulting team in the project cities prepares master plans, conducts feasibility studies and other necessary studies, prepares detailed engineering designs of the various project components and technical specifications, prepares contract documents, and supervises the project construction.

City-level committees. City-level committees are established in all RUIDP project towns for effective decision-making, coordination, and problem-solving at the municipal level. The committee is headed by the district collector and comprises elected representatives of the town, as well as senior members of all of the state line departments, such as the PHED, the electricity department, etc. The committee also helps identify subprojects, holds quarterly project review meetings, and tries to expedite construction work.

Financial Management

To simplify and expedite payments, RUIDP adopted ADB's financial disbursement systems at the program and project levels, which involve three categories: advance payments, reimbursements to the executing agency, and direct payments to the contractors. The good practices supported by this process are described in this section, including Impact Story 8.

Capacity to Spend as an Indicator of Institutional Strength, Project Management Effectiveness

As the managerial capacity of the Rajasthan Urban Infrastructure Development Project (RUIDP) has expanded, so has its systems of financial management and accounting, as well as its investment portfolio with the Asian Development Bank (ADB). That portfolio evolved from a standard project loan meant to build capacity to a multitranche financing facility (MFF), then to a sector development program. It will likely next become a line of credit for a semiautonomous urban development corporation. This trajectory will end up taking a total of 30 years.

"A good sign of financial management is when I go to Rajasthan to review the project and talk with contractors, I don't get any complaints about the timely payments. The projects are being managed well and funds are moving," said Pushkar Srivastava, senior urban project officer at ADB's India Resident Mission.

All of the first three phases have taken less time to implement than expected, although the size of the investments and the number of sites have increased. Phase 1 invested $350 million in 6 cities over 10 years, compared with phase 4, which will invest more than double that amount in 42 towns over 5–6 years. The increasing efficiency and proficiency of the program indicates that RUIDP's capacity is growing. By investing in multiple phases, ADB and the Government of Rajasthan have been able to take advantage of the capacity gained in each phase.

The capacity of an institution can be gauged according to how much money it can effectively utilize in a year.

By the end of 2019, within 20 years of its establishment, RUIDP had disbursed close to $1 billion in ADB funding for urban development. That amounted to an annual average of $50 million.

The question facing RUIDP at this point is whether it has the capacity to raise its own capital. RUIDP is now a unit of a new, larger state-level corporation: the Rajasthan Urban Drinking Water, Sewerage & Infrastructure Corporation (RUDSICO). This corporation has absorbed relevant state urban agencies with a view to streamlining urban development in Rajasthan. Its establishment is an output of an ADB-funded program loan to introduce reforms in the urban sector.

There are still a lot of questions about how RUDSICO will operate, similar to the questions people had about RUIDP during its formation. The entities that have merged into RUDSICO had been separate and independent, with their own accounting systems and structures. There is a transitional plan to align them.

Observers will be watching RUDSICO's funding sources closely, as they will be an indicator of RUDSICO's success. "Financial capacity and independent funding will be critical to the smooth operations of RUDSICO," said Vaibhav Galriya, former RUIDP project director and now the medical education department secretary for the Government of Rajasthan.

ADB is hoping that RUDSICO will be able to raise funds from its own capital investments and commercial markets. "The institution building and capacity building that happens during these projects is not as tangible as the infrastructure they build, but there are systems now in place, and the institutions are getting financially autonomous," one ADB officer observed. "The 20 years ADB has been in Rajasthan is not a long time for this kind of change."

Source: Authors.

❝ PROJECT VOICES

> **A good sign of financial management is when I go to Rajasthan to review the project and talk with contractors, I don't get any complaints about the timely payments. The projects are being managed well and funds are moving.**
>
> Pushkar Srivastava, senior urban project officer at ADB's India Resident Mission

Link Mobilization Advances to Actual Progress

Contractors have been known to divert mobilization advances (i.e., advanced payments to cover initial expenditures) to unrelated projects or to allocate only part of the advances to relevant project activities. Recovering the advances from contractors that mishandle funds in this manner can be cumbersome due to weak contractual compliance provisions. RUIDP now includes specific provisions in design-build-operate contracts concerning advance payments. The disbursement of mobilization advances is now linked to progress milestones, and is given in annual installments not exceeding 10% of the annual cost of the design-build plan; it is also limited to a 5% maximum of the overall design-and-build cost. To retrieve advance payments, RUIDP deducts 10% of each interim payment certificate. The recovery commences after 6 months of payment, while the entire amount is recovered in 18 months. In some cases, contract provisions authorize the recovery of the entire amount once 80% of the design-and-build work is completed or the stipulated period for the design-and-build work is over, whichever comes first.

Make Security Deposits Easily Cashable

To protect RUIDP from contractor defaults, RUIDP uses a nationalized bank to secure guarantees and quickly cash security deposits. Cashing contractor securities used to involve a difficult process of coordination with banks and courts in the other cities. While RUIDP would be securing the permissions to cash the bank securities, a defaulting contractor would find relief in court, causing RUIDP financial damage. In a few cases, RUIDP had to forbid the security because of these issues. Now, RUIDP demands that securities be cashable only in the project city. The exact contract language, endorsed by ADB, states that securities should be "issued by a reputable bank located in the Employer's country, which may include scheduled banks or nationalized banks, or by a foreign reputable bank outside the Employer's country, through a correspondent bank located in the Employer's country, which may include banks in Jaipur, to make it enforceable."

Provide Bonuses for Early Completion

Bonuses for finishing work early are unusual, though ADB and the state government allow them. RUIDP began using bonuses in phase 3 to incentivize the early completion of work, especially for difficult task sets such as water distribution systems, sewerage collection systems, and rehabilitation works.

The bonus is equal to the same rate they would have been penalized for each day they were delayed in completing the work; the total bonus amount is limited to 5% of the total cost of the specific task. As evidence of the effectiveness of bonuses, RUIDP can count on the work being completed early.

Procurement Management

Phase 3 was a turning point in RUIDP's procurement practices. Drawing from the experience gained during the first two phases, RUIDP management applied numerous lessons learned to its procedures and practices. "Phase 3 linked projects and contracts to performance and outcomes, and the learning curve for phase 4 has been even faster," said Manjeet Singh, former RUIDP project director and former secretary of Rajasthan's Local Self Government Department. "The fact that ULBs, with the support of RUDSICO, do their own detailed project reports in-house saves almost 2 years on total project implementation, and gives ULBs a sense of ownership." RUIDP has adopted measures to strengthen the efficiency of bidding preparations, approvals, and execution times. The program is also able to avoid delays and cost overruns during each project stage, having gained substantial savings that have been reallocated to new urban development work. RUIDP's procurement management measures are as follows:

Complete All Pre-feasibility Work before Awarding Contracts

To avoid time and cost overruns, RUIDP begins advance work immediately after the conceptualization of any subproject, and completes all pre-feasibility work before awarding contracts, including geographical and topographical surveys, all clearances and approvals, and land acquisition. Line agencies are important in assessing and securing land for subprojects. Securing land use permits for government-owned land is often more expeditious than purchasing public or private land. In any case, land assessment should be based on a 30-year need. Any clearances for land use should be secured prior to the contract award, in order to avoid implementation delays.

" PROJECT VOICES

Phase 3 linked projects and contracts to performance and outcomes, and the learning curve for phase 4 has been even faster. The fact that ULBs, with the support of RUDSICO, do their own detailed project reports in-house saves almost 2 years on total project implementation.

Manjeet Singh, former RUIDP project director and former secretary of Rajasthan's Local Self Government Department

Include in Bid Documents Detailed Guidelines for Work Scheduling

With much of the pre-feasibility work completed, next comes the bidding process. The tenders can and should include meticulous guidelines on the preparation of bids with realistic implementation schedules and costs, an accounting for climatic conditions, and a consideration of the sequential nature of multisector or bundled contracts. The PIU head and DSC experts validate the completion schedule based on the tender specifications.

Package Bids Together

RUIDP avoids multiple small contracts by using market surveys and best practices to package multiple contracts for tendering. This reduces the risks related to time, cost, inconsistent quality, and cumbersome contract management. For example, RUIDP packages water supply and sewerage works into a single contract for a whole city, also embedding 10 years of operation and maintenance (O&M) (Impact Story 9).

Impact Story 9

Pairing Infrastructure Pays Off for the Poor

The Asian Development Bank (ADB) urban investments program in Rajasthan has demonstrated how the poor can benefit from the practice of combining different kinds of infrastructure projects.

In low-income areas, narrow unpaved roads are common, and they cause blockages and stagnant water puddles that disrupt mobility; attract pests; and expose the public to poor hygiene, illness, and disease.

Many poor communities have insisted that projects include permanent roads, instead of the standard temporary access roads or construction roads that were typically built simply for transporting materials through communities to construction sites. Some communities, such as in Rajsamand, were adamant enough to block civil works until the permanent roads were built.

The ADB-funded Rajasthan Urban Infrastructure Development Project (RUIDP) began including permanent roads in its design specifications for work in or nearby poor communities. In Jodhpur, for example, new road construction was paired with drainage works in slums.

"You wouldn't recognize the place if you had seen it before," said Pushkar Srivastava, senior urban project officer at ADB's India Resident Mission. "Pairing investments in roads and drainage has helped the communities a lot."

As a result, property values in Jodhpur have risen, motivating some residents to upgrade their homes and others to sell their land.

Source: Authors.

An important lesson we learned was to include O&M—usually 10 years—in the construction contracts. This ensures quality construction and time for building local capacity before the infrastructure is turned over.

Suresh Gupta, procurement manager and deputy project director (technical) at RUIDP

Embed Long-Term Operation and Management in Contracts

During the earlier phases, RUIDP handed over the completed project works to the concerned line departments for O&M. But the lack of technical capacity within the ULBs and line departments resulted in poor maintenance of the new infrastructure, so the expected results were not achieved. "An important lesson we learned was to include O&M—usually for 10 years—in the construction contracts. This ensures quality construction and time for building local capacity before the infrastructure is turned over," said Suresh Gupta, RUIDP procurement manager and deputy project director (technical). Over several years, Gupta has led the institutionalization of many good practices in procurement and contract management under RUIDP.

RUIDP now includes long-term O&M (usually 10 years) in its construction contracts. This practice incentivizes quality construction by the contractor, who must operate and maintain the assets it has built. The contracted O&M also provides stability in the system and ensures service delivery prior to any handover to the government.

The contractors are prevented from quoting more for design and less for O&M by RUIDP's practice of setting a minimum cost for O&M, generally 10% to 20% of the total design-and-build cost. But RUIDP does allow adjustments in the O&M fees in case of any imbalances. As the ULBs and line departments become more familiar with a contractor's O&M over the 10-year period, the capacity of their own staffs will improve.

Use Performance-Based Contracting

RUIDP has adopted performance-based payments for design, construction, and O&M work. The most important and relevant indicators for the performance of a contract have been identified for each sector. For example, for the design–build (construction) phase contract payments involving a water supply project, RUIDP typically follows the payment structure whereby 50% of the payment is made once the contractor has supplied the pipe or sewer lines; 30% after the contractor has laid and joined the pipes, tested the system, and restored the construction-affected areas; and the 20% balance after the contractor has commissioned the system and met other identified performance indicators.

The change to these payment terms helped RUIDP address the frequent problem of contractor reluctance to lay and join pipes because payment for the supply of pipes had been 70%. Contractors rarely commissioned the systems on time, so road reconstruction typically dragged on, causing prolonged public inconvenience and aggravation. Linking payments to commissioning, road restoration, and actual system performance has ensured timely project schedules and a high quality of work.

For O&M-phase contract payments, RUIDP structures payments with a fixed payment of 70% within 7 days of meeting the identified key performance indicators, and the 30% balance paid within 28 days of meeting the identified indicators. RUIDP structures the contract to allow the percentage of payment needed to ensure continued operations in the event the contractor fails with regard to a few performance indicators.

Conduct Detailed Pre-bid Meetings

RUIDP sends an invitation to bid to all potential bidders, and uses a well-structured, detailed approach to pre-bid meetings and correspondence. Interested bidders are invited to an initial meeting that presents the project scope, structure, contract scope, procedure for bid submission, qualifications, contract conditions, bid document provisions, etc. And RUIDP arranges detailed and multiple site visits for prospective bidders.

The program also takes proactive measures to resolve issues regarding the qualification and selection of bidders and vendors. While it must follow the official process for the qualification of bidders and vendors, RUIDP prepares the evaluation and qualification criteria after extensive due diligence and market surveys, in order to strike a judicious balance between adequate competition and proper selection of qualified bidders and vendors. The state government, executing agency, or local authorities need experience and relevant expertise to prepare the evaluation and qualification criteria for the selection of the most suitable contractors.

Standardize Bid Evaluations

Initially, the state government formed committees within RUIDP to evaluate bids. Each committee member evaluated the documents at different stages and in a different manner. This was a labor-intensive and time-consuming process. Learning from this experience, RUIDP streamlined and standardized its bid evaluation practices to institutionalize them and make them consistent. The hallmark of the process is now the creation of specific, time-defined action plans for evaluating the bids for each tender.

Use E-tendering for Transparency and Contractor Confidence

RUIDP uses electronic tendering to assure contractors of the transparency and credibility of its bid evaluations. An e-governance system is also used in international competitive bidding to make the processes easier for both national and international bidders. Former RUIDP Project Director Naveen Mahajan (now secretary of the state's Water Resources Department) said, "RUIDP's impact on governance was felt far more due to its transparency in bidding and hiring of consultants."

Build and Maintain a Database of Contractors, Consultants, and Key Experts

RUIDP maintains a database of more than 200 potential contractors, consultants, and experts who have worked on important projects and are in good standing. The database includes performance evaluations and recommendations, and serves as a reference for future engagements. Negative performance evaluations may lead to a consultant being blacklisted. The database also keeps track of the projects that the consultants and experts are working on to avoid simultaneous works or to determine when a no-objection certificate is needed.

Project Management Capacity Challenged by Archaeologically Protected Site

The old fort in the town of Jaisalmer is a medieval marvel that attracts legions of tourists and delivers what they come for—a stroll back in time, a brush with desert mystique, and treasure shopping.

Merchants have been making their money from the past, but their future depended on an initiative by the Asian Development Bank (ADB) and the Rajasthan Urban Infrastructure Development Project (RUIDP) to usher the fort's infrastructure into the modern era.

"This has been our home from generation to generation. It is ancestral," said Bhanwari Devi, 65. The shopkeeper was born in Jaisalmer and noted that the town only began to thrive in the early 1990s, when new roads brought the old fort town out of its once-intended isolation atop Trikuta Hill.

The crowds of tourists and the new businesses that catered to them had begun to take a toll on the town's systems. Resident Bhawani Singh described the time when feces clogged the mesh-covered drains, creating a stench that would repel the tourists. Moreover, the residents had installed toilets and sinks in their homes, but did not have any connections to water supplies, wastewater systems, or drainage. Inside the walls of the old fort, there are about 500 residences, 60–70 restaurants, and 100 shops.

RUIDP began laying water and sewerage networks in Jaisalmer in 2008 and in the old fort in 2012. The project engineers suspected that all kinds of challenges would be hiding beneath the old fort, which had been designated a World Heritage Site by the United Nations Educational, Scientific and Cultural Organization (UNESCO). It is also categorized as a protected heritage site by the Archaeological Survey of India, under India's Ministry of Culture; and the ministry's standards of excavation and restoration had to be strictly followed. For instance, homes that had not been certified by the ministry were ineligible for connection to the town's systems, as they were considered to be encroachments that compromised the historical integrity of the site.

RUIDP divided the old fort into four zones, and excavated a single trench for five key infrastructure lines: water supply, sewerage, drainage, electrical, and phone.

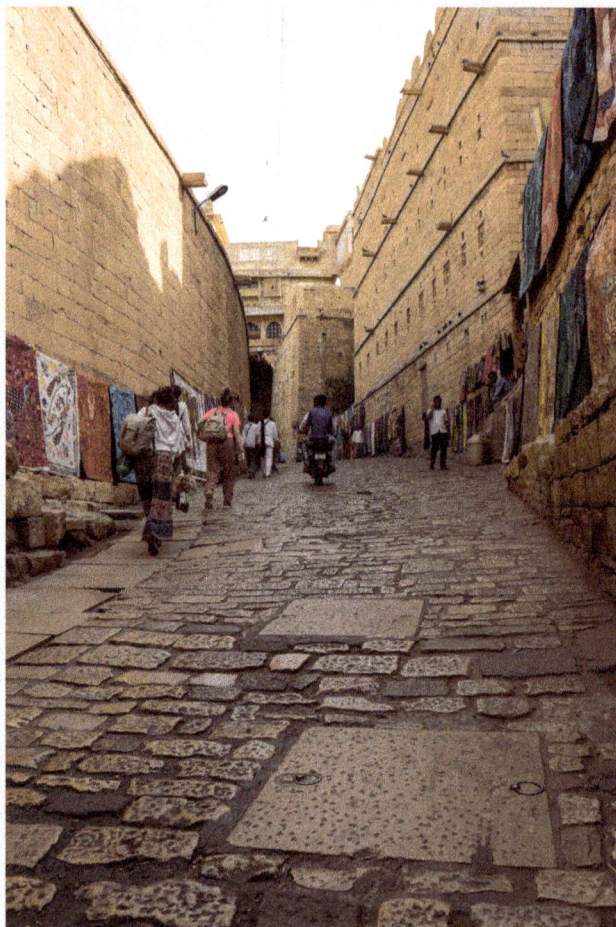

An example of strict project requirements. When RUIDP engineers laid new sewage pipes in the old fort of Jaisalmer, the new maintenance holes had to re-create the style of the sandstone originals in this 12th century UNESCO World Heritage Site.

continued on next page

Observing the changes at first hand.
Bhawani Singh (middle), his wife Rakhi (left), and his sister Sangeeta (right) stand at the doorway to their residence, which is located inside Jaisalmer's old fort. They have seen the tourist traffic increase dramatically since the ADB investments in the town's sewerage system solved the old fort's environmental problems.

The engineers met their first challenge at the old fort's entrance—an ancient, narrow, single-lane pass paved with cobblestones. It was the only working entrance to the entire fort, through which the fort's roughly 4,000 residents and all the tourists, delivery trucks, and merchants had to pass.

The second engineering challenge was the fort's shallow foundations, which reached just 2 feet beneath the heritage homes inside the fort. The excavation could not exceed 3 feet; otherwise the homes could collapse.

The third challenge was the old sewage pipes, which were only 2 feet beneath the surface and were leaking badly at the joints. To lay new pipes along the fort's steep stone slopes and narrow lanes and sharp-angled corners, RUIDP engineers excavated only the distance between maintenance holes, ensuring that each section of pipe was jointed at a maintenance hole. RUIDP laid one section of pipe between two maintenance holes each day, each section only about 49 feet long. The historic surfaces of the fort were made of soft sandstone, which had to be replaced with materials that were exact replicas of the original stone.

Resident Sangeeta Panwar, 36, said that the sewerage network has transformed the tourist traffic through the old fort. "When open sewage water used to run down the fort, there used to be a very bad odor, and the filth was seen in the open. The streets looked dirty, and the number of tourists was limited due to the narrow lanes and bad odor. The sewerage work has made the fort area clean, brought more business, and helped with better hygiene." By her count, the number of hotels in the fort area had grown from fewer than 10 to more than 40.

"People have different opinions about the interventions in Jaisalmer," said Pushkar Srivastava, senior urban project officer at ADB's India Resident Mission. "If you ask a tourist guide, he'll say the place has been spoiled. But I don't agree. We took a lot of care in installing the drainage and restoring the structures to their original condition. Now, you can walk through there and there isn't the faintest smell of sewage like before."

Source: Authors.

Implementation Management

RUIDP has fostered high-quality implementation management through the following practices:

Mainstream Community Awareness and Participation into Staffing, Design, and Implementation

RUIDP's tight-knit multidisciplinary teams are a legacy that is still clearly influencing the project during its third phase. Experts in social development, gender, poverty, and communications have permanent seats on project teams, and are in high demand by contractors and engineers.

RUIDP communication consultant Babulal Sharma is also a team leader for the Community Awareness and Participation Program (CAPP), a part of RUIDP. In that capacity, he manages consultant-based staff members specializing in gender development, poverty reduction, behavioral change communication, and community development. "The community liaison officers are an integral part of project implementation, from start to finish," he said. "Engineers really appreciate and rely on their support in the project communities."

Beginning with the design phase, the initial public consultations involve the CAPP staff along with the PHED engineers, implementation engineers, consultants, and contractor representatives.

During the implementation phase, CAPP specialists work for the city PIUs, facilitating communication between the engineering teams and the community to keep the projects moving smoothly. Nongovernment organizations (NGOs) are also contracted to help with community mobilization and awareness building.

Contractors have also improved their own communication practices. Community orientation is a part of their official scope of work for RUIDP, but contractors have also voluntarily integrated CAPP processes into their other projects, indicating RUIDP's broader impact on standard practices. Before any construction work begins, contractors engage with community outreach teams, which are headed by a social expert and NGO, to raise awareness in project communities about the scope of work, the quality standards to be expected, and the new or improved public services that will follow (Impact Story 11).

❝ PROJECT VOICES

The community liaison officers are an integral part of project implementation, from start to finish. Engineers really appreciate and rely on their support in the project communities.

Babulal Sharma, RUIDP communication consultant, team leader for the Community Awareness and Participation Program (CAPP)

Female Solidarity Mobilizes a Community

Roshan Bi was the ideal candidate for mobilizing her low-income community in the city of Tonk to support the construction of 24/7 water supply and sewerage systems by the Rajasthan Urban Infrastructure Development Project (RUIDP).

The 50-year-old widow has the only house in her community with a toilet, and her daughter was the first local female to graduate from college. Bi also has a lot of tenacity and believes in the capacity of women to get a job done.

Bi's community was the first of 35 slums in Tonk to be connected to 24/7 water supply and sewerage systems under RUIDP. A gender specialist working for RUIDP recognized these qualities in Bi and invited her to participate in the project as a community mobilizer. Bi, in turn, recruited friends.

Bi and her friends credit the reliability of RUIDP social development and gender specialist Chiranjee Lal Chandel in making them feel informed, consulted, and supported during the construction of their water supply and sewerage systems. "He went from door to door to meet with us. We had confidence in him. We trusted him. If he said it, it would happen. When he said the water was coming, we believed him," Bi said. "Even if we scolded him over something going wrong with the project, he would always come back."

The women recalled how staff from RUIDP and the Asian Development Bank (ADB), after visiting their community, would advocate for additional investments there, such as the installation of household toilets and sewerage systems. "Now we feel safe. The women have more security in the community," Bi said of the sanitation improvements.

Bi added that the RUIDP projects showed men and women in the community what they are capable of accomplishing when they have financial and technical support from programs like RUIDP. "We are cooperative and industrious. We are enthusiastic. We are already organized, too," she said. "And we have worked in the fields. So, you can imagine that we are very strong."

Women rallying support. (Left to right) Bachhi Saini, Guddi Devi, Roshan Bi, and Bi's daughter, Sama, leveraged friendships with their neighbors to garner support for ADB's investments and RUIDP's work in their low-income community.

Source: Authors.

Communities have also been involved in the implementation, monitoring, and maintenance of their new water systems. For example, during phase 3 the residents have been involved, in a highly structured way, in the operation of the new 24/7 water supply systems in their district metered areas (DMAs). Many poor communities run a community-based monitoring system, which consists of three to five residents who report problems such as leakages, and who assist other community members in making their payments on time. "The amazing part about the DMAs' implementation is that the poor communities are willing to pay for the DMAs, as long as they are satisfied with the services and the meters are working," said Srabani Sengupta, leader of the central CAPP social outreach team.

Monitor Contracts and Works with a Web-Based System

RUIDP uses Primavera software to automate its contract management and to monitor all works at the program level across multiple cities and sites. The web-based system provides real-time, multiuser monitoring and alerts that guide decision-making on corrective actions. This tool monitors each project and easily compares progress across cities. It also checks the live status of contracts and makes contract management more convenient. The system results in greater transparency with regard to progress, and saves time.

Hold Frequent Contract Review Meetings

In the early years of the investment program, an RUIDP project director institutionalized fortnightly contract review meetings, attended on-site by contractors, consultants, and engineers. Attendance was mandatory, but these meetings helped to bridge the gaps that were frequently found among these three groups.

Enforce Pre-works Safety Measures

Prior to starting any works, RUIDP requires the contractor to implement the following safety measures on-site to avoid disruptions:

- place properly sized retro-reflective warning signs on both sides of a work stretch, and have them jointly checked and verified by the PIU and DSC;
- develop a traffic diversion plan with the district administration and traffic police to minimize public inconvenience;

- arrange proper lighting and barricades at the work site to ensure night safety and convenience for the public; and
- inform the nearest hospital of planned work and the potential need for emergency medical assistance, in case an accident occurs at the site, and arrange an escape route from deep trenches in case of a mishap during an excavation.

Use Only High-Quality Construction Materials

RUIDP has adopted higher-quality materials over the years, and has used the following stringent criteria when reviewing proposed construction materials:

- superior quality, well proven, and suitable for fast construction and long-term performance;
- double wall-corrugated polyethylene pipes (long length) in sewers, instead of reinforced concrete;
- precast reinforced-concrete maintenance holes or polyethylene maintenance holes, instead of on-site construction of brick maintenance holes;
- ductile iron maintenance hole covers, instead of reinforced-concrete maintenance hole covers;
- high-density polyethylene pipes for water distribution networks, and house service connections with fusion welded saddle pipes, instead of polyvinyl-chloride or asbestos-cement pipes;
- high-standard water meters tested by the Fluid Control Research Institute;
- bulk flow meters; and
- a supervisory control and data acquisition (SCADA)-enabled water supply management system.

Reduce Delays Caused by Recurring Resubmissions of Designs and Drawings

By phase 3, RUIDP had replaced mobilization, preconstruction activities, and advance payments with service improvement programs (SIPs) for smoother project delivery and savings. SIPs may prove valuable for additional investments as well (Impact Story 12). Contractors are required to prepare a detailed SIP, which involves visiting the project sites, collecting data and creating maps, conducting surveys (e.g., topographic), and preparing designs and bills of quantities; identifying impediments; shifting utilities; and listing the required consents and permissions, potential roadblocks, etc. The design and implementation of the plans take 4–5 months, and these can be split into sub-activities with clear milestones and penalties, as well as incentives for completing work early. Contractors must finalize all their designs, drawings, and scope of work at the beginning. They can also submit their proposals for value engineering at the beginning, a preferable alternative to the common propensity of contractors to repeatedly submit new designs and drawings over the entire contract period, a practice that results in unnecessary project delays.

Minimize Road Excavations and Expedite Road Restoration

RUIDP closely monitors the road restorations in all of its infrastructure projects. The program requires contractors to restore roads within 10 days, and the total uncovered length of road cannot exceed 5 kilometers at a time. Construction activities are sequenced to minimize road excavations. And, where feasible, mechanical cutters and trenchless drilling are used. About 10% of the proposed sewer lines were laid via trenchless drilling, most often where

- lanes are as wide as 5 meters and sewer depth is more than 3.5 meters,
- traffic density is high along important roads and junctions,
- traffic diversion to other streets is not feasible, and
- there are national highway–railroad crossings.

ADB Project Efficiency Provides a Water Lifeline to Jaipur

In the early 2000s, an acute scarcity of water was forcing the Government of Rajasthan to consider moving the state capital from Jaipur, the tenth-largest city in India, with just over 3 million people.

Abandoning Jaipur due to a lack of foresight and planning would have been a costly measure.

Jaipur had been relying on two major water sources, neither of them regulated for sustainability, and scarcity was the result. The capital city then turned to the extreme extraction of groundwater. But then the groundwater levels receded into "the red zone," the point beyond which full rehabilitation is impossible.

"We use to say that Jaipur was 600% developed, meaning that we were utilizing six times the recharge rate of the groundwater," said Agam Mathur, former chief engineer at Rajasthan's Public Health Engineering Department. He now heads a busy private engineering firm that handles government and private sector projects.

For nearly 50 years, the idea of constructing Bisalpur Dam had been considered and abandoned. In 1999, the Government of Rajasthan completed the dam, but did not have the financing for water treatment plants and pipelines. Ten years later, the state government and the Asian Development Bank (ADB) agreed to allocate the savings from phase 1 of the Rajasthan Urban Infrastructure Development Project (RUIDP) to complete the water treatment plants and the transmission pipeline to Jaipur, valued at $120 million, of which ADB financed 50%, which had been gleaned from RUIDP efficiencies and savings. The works were bid for in 2005, awarded in 2006, and completed in 2008–2009.

Lifeline to Jaipur. That is what the media dubbed the Bisalpur Dam water transmission main. The media also called it the "Dream Line to the Pink City."

Source: Authors.

A new technology minimizes problems. Pali was the first RUIDP town to use trenchless technology, or horizontal directional drilling, to minimize traffic disruption, public inconvenience, and the compensation costs paid out to local businesses or residents that have encroached on easements.

If a contractor falls behind on road restoration, RUIDP places a moratorium on future construction activities, and no new work can proceed until the restoration has been completed (Impact Story 13).

Customize Capacity Building

Rather than relying on typical training formats that are used for every audience, RUIDP customizes its training events and materials, with the inclusion of project-specific and site-specific topics and issues. RUIDP has benefited from extensive and ongoing ADB-sponsored trainings that have strengthened its capacity in management and technical areas.

Over the years, RUIDP has refined its own practices as its capacity has grown with regard to procurement, consultant selection, disbursement, project management, social and environmental safeguards, and construction management. Incrementally advanced technical training has made RUIDP specialists adept at the more technical areas of urban development, such as the capture of gender equality results in operations, approaches to water demand management, municipal accounting reforms, trenchless technologies for urban projects, financial management and accounting, and contract management based on the standards of the International Federation of Consulting Engineers.

There is also, however, the persistent need to raise the capacity of the urban local bodies (ULBs) to enable them to operate and maintain the assets turned over to them by RUIDP. Neeta Pokhrel, a former ADB project officer who managed the RUIDP investments, said, "The issues of operational sustainability of assets has remained a big challenge, since the speed and level of capacity building of ULBs has not happened as envisaged. But RUIDP staff already seem to be recognizing this and are suggesting much more extensive capacity-building measures for ULBs than what was done in earlier phases."

Slow Road Reconstruction Halts Work, Delays Water

Aalima Khanam, a 16-year-old student in the central Rajasthan city of Tonk, has never had to walk several kilometers to get water and carry it all the way home on her head, like women before her. But the lack of water at home, the inconvenience, and the costly efforts she and her family endured to secure just enough water for the day had her fed up.

"I am sick and tired of this situation," she said one day in May 2018 when the temperature reached 108 °F (42 °C). "We are constantly measuring water and scheduling our life around water. Where is the water? We used to have 10 overhead tanks in this city. Now there are 18 tanks. So why is there no water?"

Tonk is one of six cities included in phase 3 of the Rajasthan Urban Infrastructure Development Program (RUIDP), funded by the Asian Development Bank (ADB). Phase 3 was designed to provide these cities with water supplies on a 24/7 basis. RUIDP had estimated that the entire city of Tonk would begin receiving pressurized, metered water from the Bisalpur Dam before the end of 2018. Until then, the city had to patiently endure the worst weeks of the dry season before the sticky monsoon rains arrived.

Temperatures increasing, but not the water. During the sweltering summer months, Aalima Khanam (left), a 16-year-old student in the central Rajasthan city of Tonk, and her sister, Sayma, 18, were anxious for the 24/7 water supply to be provided by the ADB–RUIDP project. They had invested in new plumbing and storage facilities in anticipation of the increased water supply.

continued on next page

Aalima's home is located in district metered area (DMA) 1 of Tonk, the first area in which an RUIDP contractor began constructing a new system of piped water networks and metered connections. But RUIDP representatives said that they had to tell the contractor to stop laying any further water pipes until that company had repaired the roads beneath which it had laid sewerage pipes previously. The contract has been cancelled and the work discontinued indefinitely. The inconvenience of half-repaired roads tested the public's patience. As a result, the work on the water supply networks were delayed, and Aalima's household would not have running water 24/7 for several months more.

"People have started using suction pumps. So, by the time the water should be reaching my house, there is no water," Aalima said. "One day, I got an idea, and we bought two tanks for our rooftop, and we paid a tanker to fill our storage. We pump it to the roof. We have spent thousands on tanker water here in my house."

The two rooftop tanks store about 550 liters. There are two taps in the kitchen. One tap gets water from the municipal line and the other from the overhead tanks. The family has a modern showerhead, but no one has ever used it. "My little brother had a fascination with showers, so we installed a shower for him 4 months ago. But we didn't realize that the water would vanish," she said. They had also installed a toilet few months before, but closed the flush valve when they learned how much more water flush toilets consume.

Aalima's family augments what little water they get from the Rajasthan's Public Health Engineering Department (PHED) by purchasing water for drinking and cooking from vendors, and water for cleaning and bathing from tanker trucks; and they travel to a cousin's house throughout the week to use water from the bore well on that property to wash their clothes. They spend about ₹2,800 ($40) a month on water, a major portion of which is due to the electricity needed to pump the water to their rooftop tanks.

The constant guessing as to when water will be available, and making do when there is none, has upended their household routine. They used to bathe two or three times a day, especially in the extreme dry season. Now, they bathe only once a day, which is still far more frequently than what women in other cities, like Pali, have reported.

The municipal tap at Aalima's house has flows into a 7,000-liter underground storage tank. Water used to be available enough times during the week to replenish the underground storage tank before it ever got dangerously low. But in December 2017, water from the faucet became less and less available. And once the summer dry season arrived, the reservoir went nearly dry.

Her older sister Sayma, 18, was in charge of managing the household's water supply. "She gets the most stressed about water," Aalima said. Sayma would check the water level of the underground tank at least three times a day. She kept the tap open, waiting for the sound of water.

"There is a high probably that water will come in the middle of the night because everyone is sleeping and they have turned off their water pumps," Sayma said. "We are lucky this all started after our exams, and we are on summer break." They were hoping that, by their next summer break, while the temperatures may not be any cooler, the water would finally be available on a 24/7 basis.

Source: Authors.

The capacity building for ULBs in phase 4 will be critical for the long-term sustainability of assets. "RUIDP needs to ensure that adequate mechanisms are institutionalized and in place to support and empower ULBs in their journey of taking over responsibility for local water supply and sanitation," said Vivian Castro-Wooldridge, senior urban development specialist for ADB's South Asia Urban and Water Division and the former project officer for the RUIDP investments.

Provide Neutral Multi-platform Grievance Mechanisms

To prove that public relations has a genuine value for governance, the ADB–RUIDP investments have included the establishment of long-term consumer relations centers in the project cities. RUIDP also offers the public a variety of ways to report project-related concerns, and provides faster and more transparent feedback. Technology has made much of this possible, with the development of mobile apps that allow citizens to submit complaints from their mobile devices (including photos) and to monitor the status of their complaints. The steps involved in addressing a complaint are clearly visible within the app, along with any responses and notices of resolution by RUIDP. The public may also submit complaints or concerns at RUIDP's headquarters in Jaipur or at any one of the project implementation unit (PIU) offices. RUIDP recommends engaging a neutral third party to receive and follow one's concerns through the complaint redress process, to ensure accountability, and to prevent bias. The public should also be told when they can expect responses to their complaints or requests for information.

Monitoring and Evaluation

RUIDP owes its good track record of efficient operations to its systems of quality assurance and quality control of materials and equipment, work procedures, and final outputs. Its guidelines are defined by a base monitoring and evaluation setup that enables stakeholders to compare the pre-project conditions of a city or town to the impact of the completed project. In some cases, the communities can be engaged in monitoring and contributing to the sustainability of a project (Impact Story 14). RUIDP practices are listed and described through the rest of this section.

Use Third Parties for Quality Assurance and Control

RUIDP relies on third-party quality assurance and quality control teams to monitor procedures, equipment, materials, and final output. Multiple sets of eyes on the subprojects—internally, externally, and at various management levels—ensure that any irregularities are identified early and corrected quickly. To keep all parties mindful of quality, RUIDP issues project management circulars to raise awareness about expected quality and streamlines procedures for quality control.

Use Accredited Quality Auditors

RUIDP engages third-party quality auditors to inspect all materials and manufacturing units before the materials are dispatched to the work sites. RUIDP provides the inspectors with a list of all materials and equipment likely to be procured by the contractor, descriptions of the scope of work and scope of inspection, and the design specifications. (The bid documents determine the scope of inspection.) Specialized firms with accreditation from the National Accreditation Board for Testing and Calibration Laboratories have been engaged for each kind of project.

Women in Charge of Monitoring and Repairs

Sayari Bai, in photo, is the caretaker of a community-owned tool kit for maintaining and repairing plumbing works. The tool kit contains an adjustable wrench, pipe wrench, tape for threading the pipes, and a solution for fixing seals.

She is one of several women in the neighborhood of Lohar Basti, in the city of Pali, to have been trained in monitoring local water systems and plumbing under the Rajasthan Urban Infrastructure Development Project, which is financed by the Asian Development Bank.

"When I learned I could be trained as a plumber, I was so happy," she said. It was an opportunity to contribute to her community in a practical way. Her husband died 30 years ago and her children are married and living elsewhere. She works in a flour mill on an as-needed basis, repairing the stone parts of the mill.

During the training, she learned how to tighten the pipes and elbows, and to repair leaks. Whenever people call her for repairs, she goes, never accepting any payment. Plumbing, saving people money, and saving water for her neighbors is her way of serving her community, she said.

Source: Authors.

The inspection agency is fully responsible for the quality assurance of all the materials. It confirms its assurance by embossing its identification seal on all materials it inspects and the inspection note.

If any defects are found in the materials after their receipt, the PIU informs the inspecting agency and contractor about the details of the defects, and schedules a joint inspection. If the defective material bears the inspection seal, RUIDP initiates an action against the third-party inspection agency, in accordance with the contract agreement.

The appointed quality auditors also inspect the project sites monthly and validate the quality of the work executed. Payments to the contractor are also linked to the quality of the work being done.

Closely Monitor Work with On-Site Visits

The team leader, a design supervision consultant (DSC), in consultation with the PIUs in all the project cities and towns, assigns support engineers to each subproject and deploys them to their respective project cities or towns to oversee their assigned packages. They work closely with the officer in charge at the PIU. Together, they monitor the quality of the contractor's work and the milestone time line. Their close on-site monitoring also helps ensure timely payments to the contractors.

The PIU head and DSC also regularly visit project sites during construction to ensure full compliance with the quality assurance and quality control manual; technical specifications; and other important technical, financial, and administrative parameters.

Engage Accredited Firms for Implementing Exit Protocols

RUIDP's exit protocol for turning over the ownership of all new assets to the relevant government departments relies on the highest standard of quality audits and a complete record of the project works.

The program was the first to engage firms accredited by the National Accreditation Board for Certification Bodies as quality auditors in Rajasthan. The auditors review all inspection reports, monthly test results, and verification of materials the contractor is using on-site. After all the audits are completed, the assets are handed over to the line departments.

The "as-built" drawings are important records of the salient features and locations of the new assets (sewerage networks, pipeline networks, water tanks, sewage treatment plants, water treatment plants, drains, bridges, etc.). The PIU ensures that the contractor prepares the as-built drawings throughout the execution of the project, as detailed in the contract agreement. The contractor submits these drawing for the completed parts with each running bill during project execution. The contractor then submits the final detailed as-built drawings with the final bill after completing the work, in order to secure the "taking-over certificate," which is also detailed in the contract agreement.

A complete record of the final packages is necessary for closing the contracts and the project. RUIDP submits the documentation to the line agencies and the executing agency upon the official handover, also in e-file format as an official hard copy for permanent record keeping.

Sending water. The water pipeline between Mansi Wakal Dam and Udaipur city in Rajasthan is part of an ADB-financed package that increased the city's water supply by 66%, helping to save the city's important tourism industry.

Apply Lessons Learned from Phase to Phase

As mentioned above, RUIDP works at both the program and project levels, beginning with the definition of the broad scope of the program and then the specific design work in the cities where the program is being implemented. Throughout the three investment phases thus far, RUIDP has used regular internal and external review meetings as a key mechanism for discussing issues related to contract progress, payment, approvals, etc., and for recording good practices and lessons learned, which are circulated to the PIUs so they can learn from each other. For example, contracts are reviewed together by RUIDP, the contractors, and consultants at the project management unit (PMU) level each month, and at the PIU level fortnightly. Each PIU also holds regular coordination meetings with all of the municipal line agencies to raise, resolve, and record issues; these meetings have proven key for improving future design and management. And then there are the ADB review missions for resolving issues and sharing valuable information.

"RUIDP collectively reflects on past experiences and applies those lessons," said Vivian Castro-Wooldridge, senior urban development specialist for ADB's South Asia Urban and Water Division and the former project officer for the RUIDP investments.

Healthy play. ADB investments in the facilities of the JK Lone Mother and Child Hospital in Jaipur, Rajasthan inspired the board of trustees and management to take on further capital investments, converting a courtyard that had been used for collecting waste into a covered indoor playground area, with artificial grass and natural lighting, so it can be open all year for children of families with patients.

The accumulation of experiences and insights through the phases has worked as follows:

Phase 1. RUIDP phase 1 began in 2000 with an outlay of $360 million, which was the first huge investment in the urban sector in the state. With the objective of providing integrated quality infrastructure in six large cities in the state, multiple sector projects were selected, including those concerning water supply and management, wastewater management, solid waste management, urban drainage, emergency medical services, social infrastructure, slum improvement, and infrastructure for cultural heritage sites. Given the limited investment across the sectors in the cities, the impact of the projects was very limited, with only partial improvements.

Phase 2. Drawing from the lessons learned during phase 1, RUIDP phase 2 began in 2009 with an outlay of $390 million. The focus was on improving the infrastructure in 15 selected cities to a level of visible impact. Given the needs of the cities in 2009, improvements in the bulk water facilities were considered. Phase 2 also undertook projects in other sectors, such as sewerage, solid waste, drainage, urban transport, heritage, and firefighting. Based on the experiences of phase 1, efforts were made to limit the contracts to one per sector, but 100 contracts had to be awarded to cover the required development works in the 15 project cities. Multiple contracts were awarded for similar types of work, a practice that led to severe delays, and the inter-phasing of completed works was a major concern. In many cases, the completed works were also not commissioned because various linked works had not been completed. During this phase, RUIDP also observed the capacity gaps of the ULBs when it came to operating the completed assets.

Phase 3. RUIDP phase 3 began in 2015 and is still underway, incorporating the lessons of phases 1 and 2. To improve the infrastructure and develop the capacities of institutions and the workforce, ADB and RUIDP came up with two loans for this phase: a project loan for the improvement of infrastructure in six cities, with an outlay of $250 million, and a program loan with an outlay of another $250 million, to support policy reforms and consolidate institutional development and governance improvement in the project cities. Based on earlier experiences, phase 3 is focusing on only two sectors, water supply and sewerage. With regard to water, the goal is to make supplies available 24/7, with complete coverage of each city; this entails improvements in the water distribution system and a reduction in nonrevenue water. Regarding sewerage, RUIDP aims to have 100% network coverage, along with adequate treatment systems. For more effective implementation without any hindrances, RUIDP came up with a single long-term management contract for each city—performance based and strong on operation and maintenance (O&M)—for both water supplies and sewerage. The contractor appointed in each city is responsible for both the construction of water and sewerage systems and the operation of those systems for 10 years. This provision has ensured the quality of the project works in each city.

Phase 4. With an outlay of $428.5 million, RUIDP will be incorporating the lessons learned over the prior three phases. It has proposed a single contract for each town for both the water supply and sewerage works. To minimize the inconvenience to the public, the water and sewerage works will be implemented simultaneously.

Government of India-initiated Clean India Movement (Swachh Bharat Mission). A garbage truck collects solid waste at the doorsteps of residents in the Hammir Nagar colony in Sawai Madhopur, Rajasthan. The ADB–RUIDP investments struggled to find sustainable solutions to solid waste management and at a meaningful scale within the project scope.

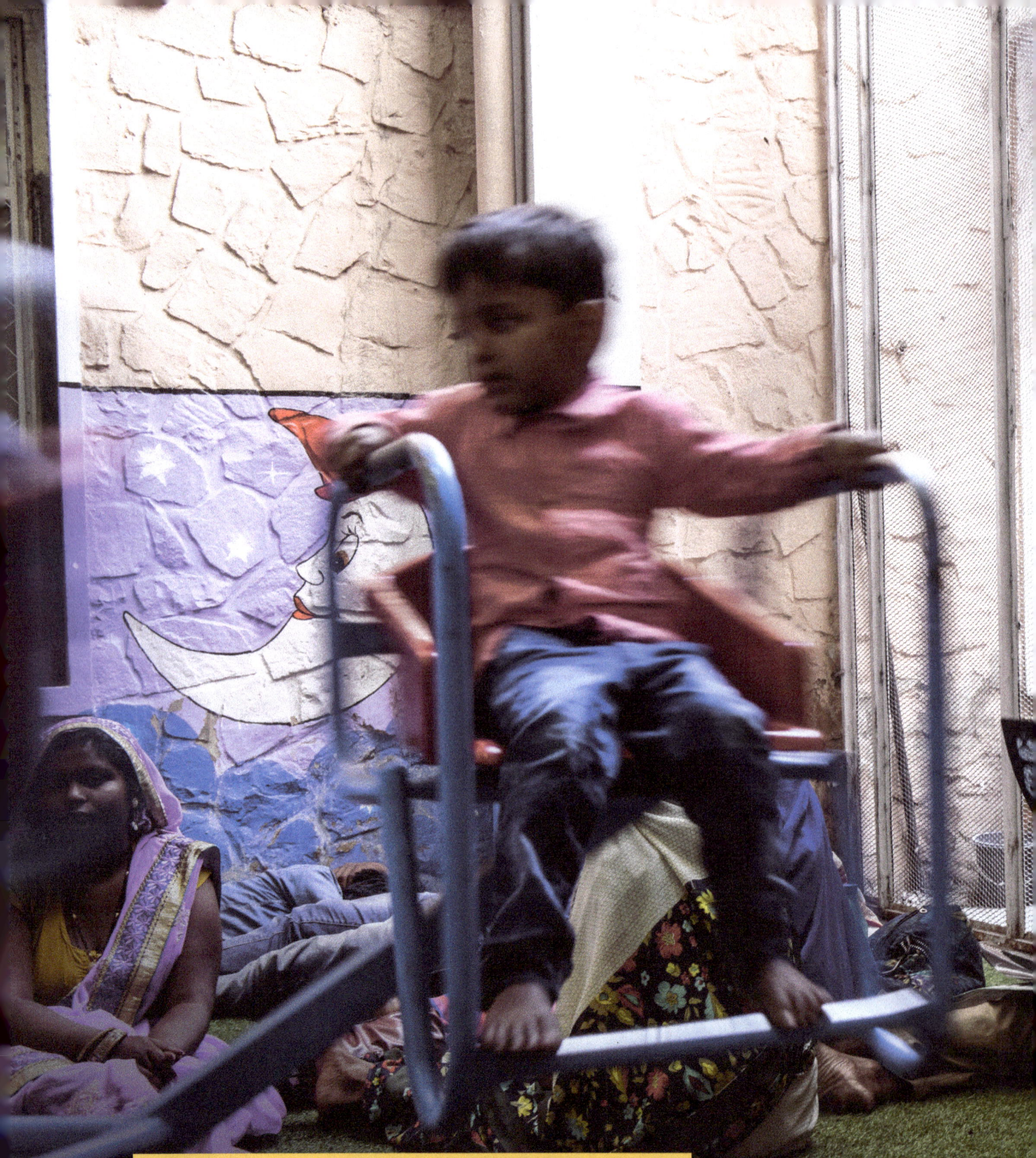

Hospital waiting room in Jaipur. ADB invested in patient receiving and waiting areas, as well as in operation theaters and intensive care wards at hospitals in Jaipur, Ajmer, Kota, and Udaipur. The investments, implemented by RUIDP, catalyzed additional renovations and services at the hospitals.

RESULTS

MORE LIVABLE CITIES

The results of the ADB–RUIDP partnership exemplify ADB's strategic vision of "livable cities," which puts the well-being of people and communities at the center of decision-making on urban development. The public health and economic crisis set off by the COVID-19 pandemic places cities at the epicenter of traumatic impact and recovery. In Asia and the Pacific, especially in India, development professionals have seen the impact of economic displacement in the cities on migrant populations and slum communities. Without safety nets in the city, migrants and poor residents are exposed to unacceptable, unlivable, and dangerous conditions that threaten their health, nutrition, safety, and even survival.

ADB's Strategy 2030 identifies "making cities more livable" as one of its seven operational priorities.[16] With COVID-19 still bearing down, this priority will guide ADB's urban operations more forcefully than ever, in order to leverage further investments for outcomes that contribute to public health and urban governance. The companion document to ADB's 2030 Strategy, the Livable Cities Operational Priority Plan, 2019–2024, sets out ADB's approach to supporting the efforts of its developing member countries to build livable cities. That approach entails: (i) improving the access, quality, and reliability of urban services; (ii) strengthening urban planning and financial sustainability; and (iii) improving urban environments, climate resilience, and disaster management. The plan also helps developing member countries create better institutions, policies, and enabling environments.[17] Altogether, ADB's goals can be summed up in the "5Es" of livable cities: (i) economic competitiveness, (ii) environmental sustainability and resilience, (iii) equity and inclusion, (iv) enabling environment, and (v) engagement. The conditions under COVID-19 will not change this course of action; if anything, they amplify its urgency. So, the 5Es will be unequivocally present in the design of forthcoming urban investments.

"RUIDP understands very clearly that its job is to make Rajasthan's cities more livable," said former RUIDP Project Director Jitendra Kumar Soni. "There are many facets of making a city livable. A city is not as livable as it can be if governance isn't what it should be. We are working on all aspects of urban development: social safeguards, governance, skills development, participatory design, sustainable infrastructure, and good service."

> By the time phase 4 is completed, ADB and RUIDP will have transformed the water situation for nearly 15 million people in 50 cities and towns across the state of Rajasthan.

In fact, the program is an elaborate case study in how to design, implement, and manage livable cities. India, as well as its neighbors in South Asia, and in Asia and the Pacific as a whole, need this case study more than ever, as urban planners and decision makers look to the future. RUIDP's results demonstrate:

- **economic competitiveness**—increased through investments in priority infrastructure (especially water supply and sanitation); urban services; and capacity building for more efficient living, commuting, working, and conduct of business;
- **environmental sustainability and resilience**—strengthened through investments that improve urban environments, such as sewerage and drainage systems, and solid waste management, as well as resilient infrastructure design, urban planning, and disaster reduction and preparedness for more adaptable, climate-ready cities;

---

[16] ADB. 2018. *Strategy 2030: Achieving a Prosperous, Inclusive, Resilient, and Sustainable Asia and the Pacific.* Manila.

[17] ADB. 2019. *Strategy 2030: Operational Priority 4; Making Cities More Livable, 2019–2024.* Manila.

- **equity and inclusion**—improved by upgrading community-based infrastructure and by officially connecting informal users to the main systems, thereby converting them into paying customers of urban services; improving access to health services; rehabilitating community assets (ponds, heritage sites, and parks); and involving marginalized groups in planning, implementation, and monitoring;
- **enabling environment**—created via the institutional development and capacity building of RUIDP, the ULBs, line agencies, executing agencies, etc., and through policy reforms and stronger urban governance, with more integrated planning and financial sustainability; and
- **engagement**—practiced by mainstreaming and mandating consultations, awareness raising, and public participation as a standard operating procedure of RUIDP throughout the project cycle, successfully demonstrating its value to contractors and engineers, who now often encourage such engagement in their non-RUIDP projects.

Economic Competitiveness

To be competitive, Rajasthan's urban economies require investments in three sectors, in particular—water supply, transport, and drainage/sewerage. Urban heritage and tourism encompass one of Rajasthan's value propositions, but cities first need major investments in basic infrastructure to support the development of the service industries that support tourism, and to absorb the waves of migrants to urban areas. The economic toll of COVID-19 on travel, tourism, and the service sector as a whole is a reminder that urban economies need to be resilient; specifically, they need supply chains and service delivery modes that can pivot quickly in times of extreme economic downturns.

Improved water supply services, expanded transport infrastructure, and the restoration of Rajasthan's urban heritage have enhanced the state's urban economies and environments. The expanded water supply infrastructure and services have brought greater equity, as systems were often extended first to slum communities and to the margins of urban areas. Roads now connect people and communities more directly to important commercial centers, employment opportunities, and to facilities providing social services (such as hospitals). The heritage restoration proved to have the least economic impact, but it did encourage inclusiveness by opening up more public spaces that the poor and upper classes can both enjoy, for instance by strolling around ponds and parks, or visiting monuments that are idyllic symbols of their shared cultural heritage.

Water Supply: The Transformation Investment Centerpiece

Water is the centerpiece of the urban investments in Rajasthan: specifically, the distribution of clean and abundant water supplies and the collection and treatment of wastewater. ADB's investments under RUIDP are continuously bringing more water to more households for more hours of the day. In addition, the water landscape is changing, with more surface water, treatment plants, transmission mains, distribution networks, and connections. By the time phase 4 is completed, ADB and RUIDP will have transformed the water situation for nearly 15 million people in 50 cities and towns across the state.

Urban Investments Put City Back on the Map, Ready for Competition

Even in this age of urbanization, Chittorgarh's population was declining. It shrank by 20% from 1991 to 2001, and then by 16% from 2001 to 2011, though the city's density was increasing. In 2006, the Ministry of Panchayati Raj named Chittorgarh one of the country's 250 "most backward districts" (out of a total of 640). It is one of the 12 districts in Rajasthan receiving support from the Government of India's Backward Regions Grant Fund.

Chittorgarh's "backwardness" is somewhat ironic, given the fact that this southeast Rajasthan city has a history of going to extraordinary engineering lengths to secure itself. The 7th century Chittor Fort, the largest fort in India, is known as the "Water Fort" for the 4 billion liters of water it once held in ancient human-made ponds and wells. About 40% of the 200-acre fort was dedicated to water storage. But today the fort is of little use to the modern city that sprawls below. When the Asian Development Bank (ADB) and the Rajasthan Urban Infrastructure Development Program (RUIDP) entered the picture, modern Chittorgarh's raw water storage and supply networks were failing to serve the needs of much of the city's population.

Chittorgarh is located on the banks of the Gambhiri and Berach rivers. In 2011, nearly 160,000 people were living there, and almost 40% of them lacked access to piped water. When ADB and RUIDP threw a financial lifeline to the municipality, the leadership found a solution for raw water storage in a nearby abandoned quarry.

First a quarry, now a dam. By utilizing an abandoned quarry as a dam, the ADB-financed water supply project in Chittorgarh was able to increase the city's water supply by 30%. A nearby cement factory, a major employer on Chittorgarh's outskirts, benefits from the reservoir, as do the surrounding residential and commercial areas.

continued on next page

The ADB–RUIDP investment financed the diversion of Berach River waters into the quarry, transforming it into a reservoir for the city. ADB also financed a second intake well, three pumps, a water treatment plant, and networks, as well as connections for the outlying areas of the city. Chittorgarh is now supplying the 7.5 million liters of water per day that it needed for the 40% of the population that had been living without.

One area on the outskirts, not far from the quarry, was receiving the quarry water and started growing rapidly; a new cement factory soon opened its doors there. The cement plant employs many of the local residents. People on the streets surrounding the plant often wear hard hats, returning home every day weary and dusty. Mazes of markets and vendors now surround the cement factory to cater to them.

Unfortunately, the homes of laborers and their families, and the maze of markets and vendors that have crowded into this part of town, illustrate the misaligned nature of urbanization. In India, urban infrastructure is rarely equipped to absorb the population of migrant workers that the cities' industries need and will attract. One of the necessary elements of economic growth ends up on the back burner, and it is usually infrastructure. As a result, cities tend to hobble along, just getting by until an investment, such as ADB's, gives their infrastructure the boost it needs. But before that happens, it is a case of urban retrograde.

Chittorgarh's backwardness may be coming to an end, however. The city's connectivity is growing. The completed Golden Quadrilateral Road Project and North–South and East–West Corridor expressways pass through Chittorgarh, connecting it to much of the rest of India. And the city is the site of a major train depot, so it has direct rail links to all the major Indian cities. ADB has also financed a new, fully outfitted fire station, a sewage treatment plant with a distribution system and household connections, and critical roads that connect key parts of the city and divert the traffic that used to clog railroad crossings.

"This project had the right alignment of politics and RUIDP," said Babulal Sharma, director of the Community Awareness and Participation Program, under RUIDP.

Source: Authors.

When ADB began investing in Rajasthan, in 1998, the state's Public Health Engineering Department (PHED) could only provide most cities and towns with water for an hour or two every couple of days. Residents invested in underground tanks to store water whenever it was flowing from the tap. Booster pumps were cheap and readily available, and house after house suctioned water from the pipes, vying with their neighbors, to coax the water flow and diminishing the water pressure in adjacent homes. In fact, they still do that in areas where ADB and RUIDP have not yet been at work.

Still Incomplete, Yet Already Transformational

Over the three phases of ADB investments so far, the goal for water provision has become bolder: from 1 hour every day in phases 1 and 2 to 24 hours every day in phase 3. According to a 2013 World Bank-funded water sector assessment of Rajasthan, the majority of towns and cities were receiving water at least once every day.

Pali—Ground Zero for 24/7 Water Supplies

The Rajasthan Urban Infrastructure Development Project (RUIDP) commissioned its first 24/7 water supply system in 2017, in one of the poorest communities in the city of Pali: Lohar Basti.

"It was unbelievable to them that they would get 24/7 water," said RUIDP's community liaison, Devendra Singh. "They thought it was impossible."

The name Lohar Basti implies that the residents were once upon a time, not too long ago, born to be blacksmiths and were poor. Most still have pre-industrial jobs such as carrying stones at construction sites and other odd, unpredictable labor that they can find day to day.

The poorest communities in the project cities are usually the first ones where RUIDP has built and connected water and sewerage systems, whether during in the earlier phases of the program, when RUIDP was just augmenting the water supply to add a few more hours a week, or in the later phases, when 24/7 water supply became the engineering and service norm.

In Lohar Basti, Sangeeta Lohar, 16, has been taking care of her household since she was 6 years old. She used to spend her whole day walking back and forth to the community tap. When her house was connected to the water supply system, she said, her entire life changed.

"I feel better now. I don't have all the aches and pains from carrying water all of the time," she said. Sangeeta had also been living with constant stomach aches caused by the not very clean water she drank from the old source, but she has not felt those cramps since getting her household connection to the new system.

A blue drum that was once used for storing water is now a makeshift table for the earthen pot that keeps the tap water cool. Her home is tidy, and she has more time to sleep at night and rest during the day. Also, for the first time in her life, she has free time for herself.

"I took [part in] a self-help group and learned how to sew," she said. "If I didn't have this water connection, I would not have the time to sew."

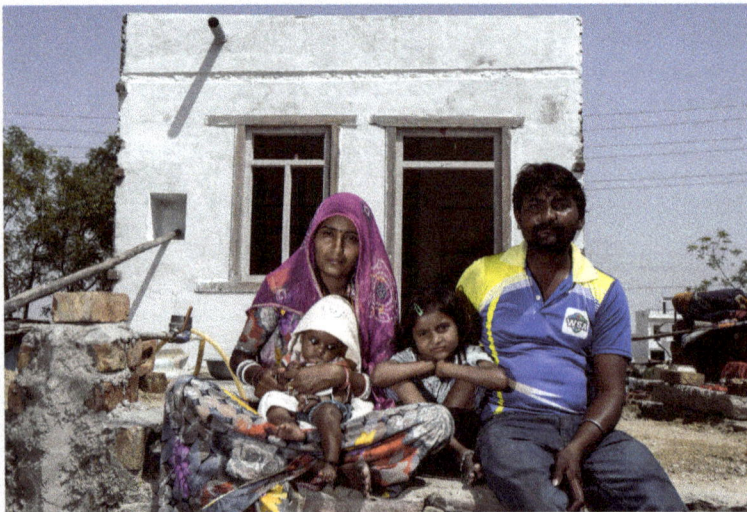

A water connection in a new home.
Ramesh and his wife, Rekha, began building their home within months of securing a water connection. "We were determined to build a house because we suffer during the monsoons," Ramesh said.

continued on next page

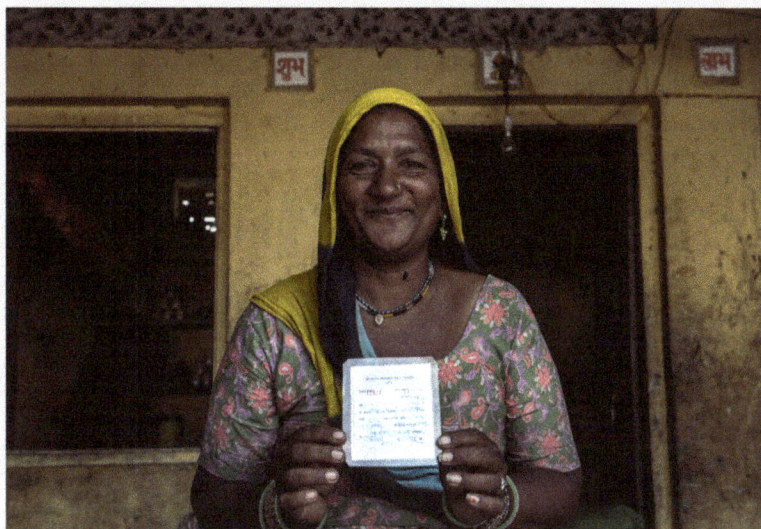

Getting a legal water connection.
Their neighbor, Rekha, once rigged a free illegal connection, but preferred to pay for a regular, legal one. She is now installing a toilet and bathroom in her house.

Across the unpaved road in front of Sangeeta's house, Bhanwari Devi, 65, and her daughter, Santosh Devi, 35, were one of the last households in the community to be able to afford the modest connection fee.

"Before the connection, we were even careful about how much water we drank because of all the work in getting the water," Santosh said. "I'm sure we were weaker then."

They borrowed and saved for six months to be able to pay the connection fee for the water supply.

"When I got this connection, I was able to work more on the construction site," Santosh said. Before the connection, she worked about 15 days a month. Since getting the connection, she has been working 20–25 days per month. She earns ₹250 per day (less than $4) for carrying stones for 10 hours. The extra days of work have boosted her income by as much as 65%.

In the low-income community of Sansie Basti, also in Pali, Ramesh, 36, and his wife, Rekha, 30, began building their home within months of securing their water connection. "We were determined to build a house because we suffer during the monsoons," Ramesh said. He and his wife both work in construction jobs.

Ramesh and Rekha moved to Sansie Basti in 2011. The government gave them the title to a plot of land in 2015. They received a water connection in 2017, and began building their home in 2018. With the water connection, Ramesh said, "I have saved time and money. Without this, I would have to get water delivered from a tanker truck." He estimated that he would have needed to purchase 15 water tanker truck deliveries to build the house if he did not have the connection on his property. They pay about ₹80 per month for a piped water supply, at ₹2.25 per 1,000 liters. The 3,000-liter delivery of water from a tanker truck cost ₹500—a 99% savings.

When their neighbor, Rekha, 40, had rigged an illegal connection, it was treated as a free-for-all by everyone in the community, "but we were always ready to pay for the water if the connection was there," the neighbor said. She has since begun installing a toilet and bathroom in her house.

Source: Authors.

The goal for phases 1 and 2 now appears to be relatively modest, yet it was actually transformational. The phase 1 investments generated an additional 641 million liters per day (MLD) of water, thereby providing improved water supplies to 7 million people in the six largest cities in Rajasthan.[18] Phase 2 provided 1.6 million people with improved water supplies in 15 medium-sized towns (covering 85% of the towns' total population). In the desert town of Jaisalmer, for example, the construction of new raw water storage facilities increased the municipal water reserve by 15 days, and reduced the residents' time accessing potable water from more than 2 hours per day to less than 15 minutes. This was especially transformative for women, who are the primary water managers for their households, and for the poor, who often endure greater drudgery accessing water than people who live in more centrally located communities and have more convenient and affordable options for securing water.[19]

In addition, an ADB independent evaluation confirmed that the installation of sewerage and drainage systems reduced the mosquito populations, poor aesthetics, and damage to roads in the project cities.

Water 24/7

By phase 3, the investment strategy regarding water supplies shifted radically. Five project cities would demonstrate the viability of systems delivering water on a 24/7 basis. The systems require reliable water sources (especially in dry season), entirely new piping from end to end, new management systems and technologies, and meters.

The new systems also require that each city be divided into zones, and that each zone be further divided into four or five district metered areas (DMAs). The DMAs are themselves divided into four or five "step areas," each with 400–500 households. The DMAs are hydrologically isolated from one another, with a bulk meter at the network inlet to record pressure and volume, as well as domestic water meters throughout each step area. The system enables utility managers (typically from the PHED or private contractors) to monitor, detect, and quickly resolve issues, such as leakage or pilfering.

The volume of nonrevenue water loss averages more than 50% in non-rehabilitated systems in Rajasthan. ADB expects the new DMA-based systems to lose only 7% at the DMA level and 15% at the city level. Those are the targets for the contractors that design, install, and monitor the systems. The first DMAs commissioned by RUIDP reported nonrevenue water loss at 5.9%, down from 40% before the project. Water that would have been lost in the old system have now effectively become a new supply.

After a DMA is commissioned, RUIDP and the local PHED office work together, first to disconnect the local households from the old system and connect them to the new, and then to stabilize the usage rates. After that, RUIDP will turn the new system over to the local ULB office. As owners of the assets, the local ULB offices operate and maintain their systems or hire a private firm to do so, typically offering long-term contracts.

---

[18] ADB. *Completion Report: for Rajasthan Urban Infrastructure Development Project (Tranche 1)*. Manila. The 641 MLD of additional water supplies is the sum of 184 MLD of water augmented in Jodhpur, Kota, Bikaner, and Udaipur; 57 MLD from 190 tube wells installed in Jaipur; and 400 MLD of water from the Bisalpur Dam.

[19] Women and children are responsible for collecting and storing water in nearly three-fourths (70%) of households surveyed for the midterm impact assessment study of the RUIDP phase 2 investments.

The ULBs do not have much experience in working with the private sector in the operation and maintenance (O&M) of public services, but in phase 3 RUIDP project implementation have opened the door to private contracts for the O&M of new water and sewage works. By the completion of phase 3, all water and sewage works will be under private management and all of them are through contracts lasting 10 years.

Once RUIDP completes the construction or installation of assets and the testing of them, it turns the assets over to the relevant local body. The first DMAs to be developed have been in slum communities, the most water-disadvantaged areas in any city. The convenient, clean, 24/7 water supply has motivated residents to invest in more permanent housing and sanitation facilities. In the first DMA to be established in Pali, the government has begun categorizing slums as permanent residential upgraded areas. Communities are also becoming eligible for other national housing and community development programs. (The social and economic changes that poor communities have experienced because of RUIDP is explored in further detail in a later section of this chapter, "Equity and Inclusion.")

Designs Should Not Assume the Existence of Connections

Post-project evaluations found reasons for concern about the sustainability of some of the water supply and sewerage infrastructure. The challenge for former RUIDP Project Director Vaibhav Galriya (now commissioner of the Jaipur Development Authority) during his tenure was getting people connected to the sewerage network, he said. In some cities, government had invested in the installation of sewer lines, but had not connected any users. And the initial program design, cost, and construction contracts did not include the connections. "People didn't feel the need to connect," Galriya said. "RUIDP had a huge role to play in their change of mindset, and now the public demands these systems."

> ## " PROJECT VOICES
>
> ### People didn't feel the need to connect. RUIDP had a huge role to play in their change of mindset, and now the public demands these systems.
>
> Vaibhav Galriya, former RUIDP project director and now commissioner of the Jaipur Development Authority

ADB had financed the sewerage networks, the maintenance holes, and treatment plants. This was already a more comprehensive approach than was common in the development era gone by, when banks and governments built wastewater treatment plants all over Asia, assuming that the networks would get built by the governments, as they were the more affordable parts of the system. But the networks were never built, and treatment plants have become relics of faulty development thinking; they are now regarded as object lessons in the development literature.

Moreover, with both the networks and treatment plants in place, the assumption was that the residents would want to connect with them. But they did not want to connect, and the municipal governments were faced with a dilemma: they could wait for the state government to allocate more funds, so they could pay for the connections themselves (something they could not manage on their own), or they could impose connection fees on their constituents (which could have political repercussions).

The RUIDP leadership was hesitant to finance the connections from program funds because other cities were still waiting for the program to reach them. "Communities have called our office, called their officials, called the city collector, and their city committee members demanding to know, 'When are you connecting our area?'" said Anil Vijayvargiya, executive engineer for RUIDP's Sawai Madhopur project implementation unit (PIU).

The state government received nearly $250 million in incentive-based stimulus financing from ADB upon its completion of the reform program outlined in ADB's program loan. Eventually, RUIDP did allocate some of these funds to covering the connection costs in project cities and to expanding sewerage system coverage to 100% of project city residents.

The forthcoming phase 4 investments will propose that all construction contract packages include free household connections in areas with sewerage systems to ensure immediate and adequate flows to sewage treatment plants.

Transport: Roads That Drive Connectivity, Efficiency, and Opportunity

The urban investments in Rajasthan have built roads and bridges in more than 20 of the state's most economically important cities, which also have the largest concentrations of poor communities. More than 3 million people are benefiting from the new roads and bridges that ADB financed and RUIDP built.

From 1998 to 2014, the investments supported the:
* preparation of comprehensive master plans to guide transportation- and traffic-related investments and activities in the project cities;
* construction of 20 bridges and roads that eliminated intersections at railroad crossings by moving traffic either over or under the railroad tracks, reducing the average crossing time from up to 15 minutes to less than 2 minutes;
* resurfacing of 10 roads that are major routes to project cities, thus helping to relieve the traffic congestion within cities and improve the residents' mobility and travel times; and
* the construction and/or rehabilitation of 215 kilometers of roads, two bridges, and several rail over bridges.

New Roads and Bridges Eliminate Railroad Chokeholds in Cities

India's ubiquitous railroad infrastructure is a century old, and though rail is still an important means of transporting people and cargo (including bulk water supplies between some Rajasthan cities), railroad crossings can jam up a city's traffic flow. The length of the railways in Rajasthan is equivalent to only a fraction of the total length of the state's roads: 5,893 kilometers of rail compared with 217,701 kilometers of road. Yet railway crossings hold large urban areas hostage at all hours of the day. Below are examples of how projects financed by the Asian Development Bank (ADB), under its Rajasthan Urban Infrastructure Development Project (RUIDP), have solved the problem of congestion at railroad crossings in cities in Rajasthan.

In Bikaner, one of the state's larger cities, eight railroad crossings cut through the northeast section. Some of these crossings intercept national highways, and two of them are only 40 meters apart. The crossings were closed an average of 54 times per day for 15–20 minutes, backing up traffic for half a kilometer in both directions. In fact, the crossings were closed more than they were open. Bikaner had only one "rail over bridge" (ROB), which is a road bridge over a railway track.

That ROB forms part of the national highway, and it improves the connectivity between Bikaner and Jodhpur, another major city in Rajasthan. Heavy load-bearing trucks are allowed to use the ROB at night. Also, like all ROBs, the one in Bikaner has footpaths.

ADB investments constructed two 900-meter long, four-lane ROBs, which a total of 100,000 passenger vehicles cross daily. Because of the heavy traffic at the railroad crossings, the railway department covered some of the costs of the two new ROBs. Five railway crossings in Bikaner are still operating without ROBs, so they are potential targets for future road network investments.

Rail over bridges. All modes of transport ply the streets of Rajasthan's cities. The ADB-financed RUIDP has built several "rail over bridges," including one on Bikaner's Gajner Road (above). Motorists and other travelers can now bypass congested railway crossings.

continued on next page

In Chittorgarh, some neighborhoods were cut off entirely from the rest of the city because their only access was over a railroad crossing that was closed up to 6 hours in a day, to allow the passing of about 30 trains. The only alternative route was a 40-minute detour. But ADB has financed the construction of a new road under the railroad bridge.

Moolsingh Bhatti, 46, of Chanderia village, in Chittorgarh district, once waited up to 20 minutes for the crossing to open at Chanderia Station. Now he zips along the new road on his motorcycle, confident that he will arrive on time at the dairy farm where he works.

"I know I can reach work in less than 20 minutes and even earlier," he said. "But it's the auto rickshaws that have benefited the most from this road."

The auto rickshaw drivers also use—and earn more money from—a variety of new routes accessible from the recently built Chanderia underpass.

The underpass has generated a number of indirect benefits. Fire trucks and ambulances can now reach more areas of the city much faster. The general area is also more passable in the monsoon season because of new drainage infrastructure around the road. And property values are on the rise, as indicated by the orderly stakes in the ground along both sides of the new road.

In Udaipur, the addition of a lane to the Ayed Bridge more than doubled the number of passenger cars that crossed the bridge in a day.

In Rajsamand, a narrow unpaved access road to farmland was expanded and paved to provide a more direct route to government administration buildings. The road now also provides a new exit from the city for a number of bypass roads.

The newly expanded road has led to the conversion of farmland into more spacious residential and commercial development. Mufaddal Hussain, 32, who owns a hardware store, moved his business to the area to take advantage of the booming construction. He also lives nearby.

"Farmers were the only ones who used to use this road. Now look. A lot of new markets have popped up along this road, and there's all that new housing development there on the other side," he said. "For businesses, there is more space for parking, and I have twice the floor space to display merchandise and keep inventory."

An improved road attracts businesses. A newly expanded and paved road in the city of Rajsamand, financed by ADB under RUIDP, has permitted the construction of more spacious commercial properties and customer parking, which have, in turn, attracted shopkeepers like Mufaddal Hussain, who moved his hardware store to the new road.

Source: Authors.

Urban Heritage Restoration: Capitalizing on Rajasthan's Historic Sites

During the design consultations for the first phase of the RUIDP investments, ADB and RUIDP found a way to make the infrastructure packages more attractive to the municipalities that would be borrowing to implement them.

Stakeholders had expressed a strong interest in restoring historic gates, ancient step wells, monuments, parks, and ponds that were falling into disrepair, crumbling into history. Municipal and civic neglect had led to their poor condition. Heritage restoration is not likely to receive public budget allocations, yet they fit nicely into the multisector approach to the RUIDP investments.

"We tend to attach a negative connotation to 'political decisions,' like incorporating these kinds of projects in what is essentially an infrastructure project," said Preetam Yashvant, former RUIDP director. "Still, what is a political decision but a representative wish of the people? This is how these kinds of investments, like cultural heritage restoration, are included. They are an entry point to gaining people's trust."

The heritage restoration sites were chosen in a series of major public consultations. (The sites protected by the Indian Archaeological Society were not eligible.) The selections for restoration, located in 10 cities, included fort walls, city gates, step wells, temples, forts, palaces, and monuments. The costs were low compared with the massive outlays for infrastructure work, yet the impact would be enhanced by the broad public support, especially for the recreational spaces that were created. Grounds were lit and outfitted with public toilets, rubbish bins, and sidewalks. The aged and weathered facades were blasted with chemicals and re-plastered.

Complicated work. Heritage restoration turned out to be complicated and unfamiliar work for the civil engineers at RUIDP. "Everyone wanted to do it right, and this was more specialized than anything," said Ashok Srivastava, a RUIDP staff member who later became a senior urban project officer at the ADB India Resident Mission. "For example, Jaipur is known as 'the Pink City.' There is a paint color everybody calls "Jaipur Pink," but there are a thousand shades of Jaipur Pink. So which Jaipur Pink are we to use?"

RUIDP had to call on the *rajmistris,* the old artisans who are now back in their villages, to discuss how things must be done. RUIDP found them by word of mouth, mainly through contractors. The *rajmistris* were hired to supervise the masons and other contractor jobs, but they speak a dialect unknown to most RUIDP engineers, so translators had to be hired.

The program pulled up more chairs to the table, as more people were required to understand, execute, and supervise the work. RUIDP consulted with the Archaeological Survey of India and the Department of Archaeology and Museums of Rajasthan. Other heritage experts, conservation regulators, and specialized architects were called to Jaipur and to the nine other cities across the state where heritage restoration work would be done.

The published government rates for construction were not appropriate for the specialized work. New cost schedules were developed for preparing the bids. The cities and departments used RUIDP's rate schedule and technical specifications for heritage conservation work. In the end, Jaipur's entire army fort was restored according to RUIDP's technical specifications and rate schedule.

A view of Jaipur from the Wind Palace.
In Jaipur, the ubiquity of "Jaipur Pink" is manifest in the facades of buildings, historical monuments, forts, and palaces. But there are several shades of Jaipur Pink, and determining the actual shade of pink needed for the restoration of each heritage site was an unexpected challenge for the Rajasthan Urban Infrastructure Development Program (RUIDP).

In ruins. Open sewage water used to run down the ancient walls of Jaisalmer Fort; there used to be much bad odor and the filth was seen in the open. The streets looked dirty and the number of tourists were limited due to narrow lanes and bad odor. The sewage work has made the fort area clean, brought in more business, and helped in better hygiene.

It was a challenge, but one that most people agree was worth it. The projects generated goodwill and bought time while the water supply, sewerage, and transport infrastructure components were ramping up.

A Lesson in Maintaining Restored Heritage Sites

The potential value of the rehabilitated heritage sites was immense, and nobody objected to being included in the program's scope. Jaipur receives the second-largest number of tourists in the country, after Agra (in Uttar Pradesh), home of the Taj Mahal. Of all the official heritage sites in India, 25% are in Rajasthan.

"The ADB–RUIDP investments started a trend," said Srivastava. "There wasn't any conservation work happening in Rajasthan before this project."

But did the heritage restoration improve the economy of the cities? A perception survey carried out by ADB and RUIDP of 110 respondents suggests that the tourist flow and business activity increased only marginally as a result of the heritage restoration. In several cases, the restored heritage properties have not been well maintained and the intended benefits are not evident. The facades of fort walls and gates have succumbed again to rot from monsoon dampness and glued-on bits of campaign posters. The stepwells and ponds are choking again on debris and sludge that have escaped from somewhere.

Heritage sites that enjoyed more protection have fared better, such as in Bikaner, where the cultural heritage conservation work at Sursagar was found to have significantly improved the quality of life of the residents and increased nearby property values. Several restored gates scattered around Jaipur have added glory to their functionality, and architectural iconography to the famed city's streets.

The poor upkeep of some of the heritage sites is disappointing and puzzling. It has raised questions about the division of responsibilities between the citizens and their government: should the public wait for politicians to act, though they may be motivated by upcoming elections or simply their whims? Or should citizens volunteer to take responsibility for the heritage sites in their midst? Where would that sense of civic duty come from? Does it still exist? Or is it a thing of the past, of a time when people depended less on the government, and more on each other? Cities differ from villages in terms of their social structures and social forces. Their landscapes are far more varied, too. But the fact that historic monuments and buildings have been allowed to deteriorate before the loans for their restoration have even been paid off goes against economic rationality. Even in cases where grant money had enabled the restoration, the poor upkeep of the heritage sites demonstrates the need for capacity building among municipal managers and for behavioral change among the members of the public who visit these sites.

The lessons learned regarding the maintenance of restored landmarks have resulted in greater resources being allocated to the development of a sense of engagement on the part of the public, and to awareness raising and capacity building for municipal leaders. The investments in phase 3 were also redirected to more traditional areas of multisector lending: water, sewerage, and drainage.

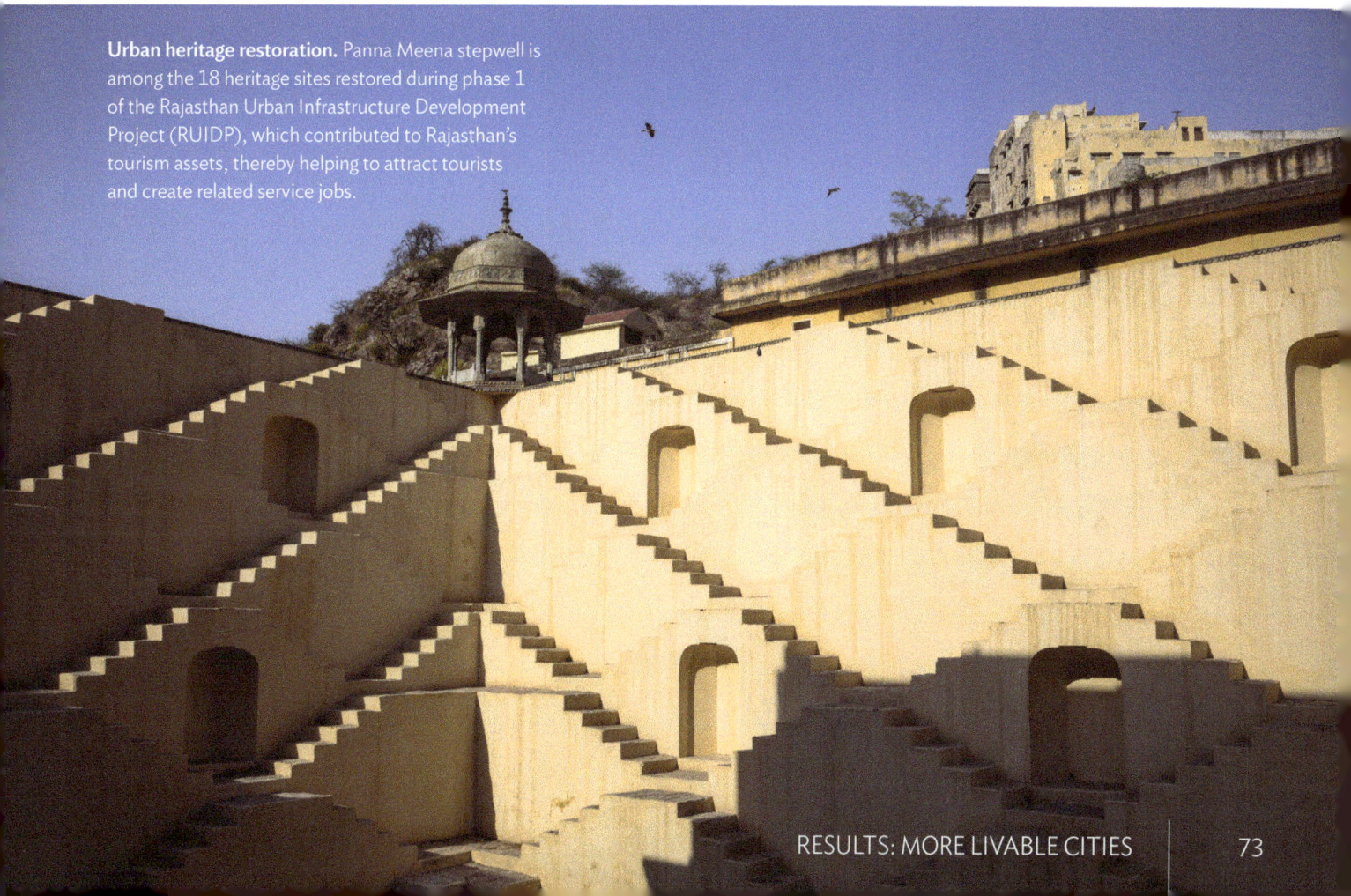

Urban heritage restoration. Panna Meena stepwell is among the 18 heritage sites restored during phase 1 of the Rajasthan Urban Infrastructure Development Project (RUIDP), which contributed to Rajasthan's tourism assets, thereby helping to attract tourists and create related service jobs.

Urban heritage restoration. Jaipur's Ajmer Gate is among the 18 heritage sites restored during phase 1 of the Rajasthan Urban Infrastructure Development Project (RUIDP), which contributed to Rajasthan's tourism assets, thereby helping to attract tourists and create related service jobs.

Lack of Maintenance Threatens the Future of Restored Heritage Sites

The cities of Rajasthan, big and small, are dotted with ancient human-made ponds built by *maharajas* to collect rain for drinking water. The ponds, like stepwells, were considered to be "common property resources," but when they were first constructed, centuries ago, there was less pressure on them in terms of use. Communities also maintained them zealously because they were critical sources of water, and thus their life-support systems.

The upkeep of the ponds has lapsed in many cities since then. Encroachment and alternative water sources have led residents to disregard the ponds, allowing them to fill up with unchecked pollutants and solid waste.

That was the case with Sursagar Pond, in Bikaner. Elected ward counselor Krishna Shekhawat, 59, said that local residents her age remember avoiding the pond when they were growing up. "We used to pass the [pond] without so much as looking at it. The smell was so foul, it was difficult to breathe," she said.

Sursagar is located in front of Bikaner's main attraction, Junagarh Fort. Built in 1614 by Maharaja Sur Singh to collect rainwater, the pond has a surface area of almost 23,000 square meters, and a depth of 8 meters. It was rehabilitated during phase 2 of the Rajasthan Urban Infrastructure Development Program (RUIDP), funded by the Asian Development Bank (ADB). Back in the days when Sursagar was still polluted, tourists visiting the nearby Junagarh Fort would sometimes wander down there. They still go there today, but back then, said Shekhawat, it was embarrassing to watch their reactions to the pond.

The municipal government initiated boating operations after the rehabilitation, but they have not been profitable. The paddleboats are turned upside down on an embankment and the paddles are rusting.

The bad old days of Sursagar Pond. Krishna Shekhawat, an elected ward counselor, said that local residents her age remember avoiding Sursagar Pond while growing up, but ADB investments have given the city a chance to appreciate the ancient pond again.

continued on next page

Across the state, attempts to promote boating and other recreational activities in these ponds have failed to generate revenues. There is no sense of public ownership of the ponds, as there was centuries ago, when they were vital sources of water for the communities, rather than just an aesthetic or recreational asset. Moreover, the local bodies responsible for the ponds, whether municipalities or trusts, have not received sufficient funding to operate and maintain the equipment and facilities."

Sohail Khan, 16, is paid a monthly wage of ₹4,000 (just over $53) to paddle around the pond for almost 12 hours a day, clearing out floating debris with a makeshift net on the end of a bamboo pole.

Sursagar may smell better and look better than it did 10 years ago, but the long hours Khan has spent working there have given him a few ideas for further improvements. He would drudge up the pond every year to keep it truly clean. He would buy new boats and make sure they were maintained this time; and that would include washing the bottoms of the boats. He would add more lighting to keep the premises safer at night. And he would paint Rajasthani images or cartoon characters on the blank, peeling walls around the pond.

"Most people come here at night to drink," he said. "And when I tell them that it's not allowed, they want to fight." He is not paid to fight for Sursagar, he said, so every morning he ends up removing 10 to 15 empty bottles from the pond.

Khan works at this job because he can send his salary home to his parents, who live 30 kilometers outside the city on a farm.

If the operation and maintenance of Sursagar Pond is not strengthened, it could end up like a heritage pond in Bundi that is been rehabilitated, but is now on the decline.

Keeping the lake clean. Sohail Khan is paid ₹4,000 a month to paddle around the rehabilitated Sursagar Pond for almost 12 hours a day, clearing out the floating debris.

continued on next page

Tourists have long been coming to Bundi to see the miniature paintings for which the city is famous. In addition, one of Bundi's most famous landmarks is the 17th century Bundi Palace, which appears to have been carved into the hill that looms over it.

Rajat Tailor, 27, spent his childhood in the shadows of Bundi Palace, surrounded by tourists. "I loved talking to them," he said. "I learned English that way."

At the foot of the palace is Naval Sagar Pond. ADB invested in a drainage system around the pond, and in other structural and cosmetic fixes to boost tourism. The ADB investment was able to rid the pond of its stench and pollution. For a while it remained pristine, but its rehabilitation has been flagging due to inadequate maintenance by the urban local body.

It was his experience with this site that inspired Tailor to earn a master's degree in tourism management. "Bundi is not a famous place," he said, explaining his decision. "But the tourists that do come like that it is small and quiet and not expensive."

The pond should be a prime strolling ground for townspeople and the tourists staying at the surrounding hotels. A boating enterprise, initiated to leverage the ADB investment, was operating until the stench returned and was too offensive to attract boaters. "Tourists always tell me, 'This is beautiful. You should keep it clean,'" said Tailor. "But the people also have to do something about this."

Responsibility for Bundi's heritage. Rajat Tailor, who grew up in Bundi, is disappointed by the lack of maintenance of the heritage sites around the city. He believes that both the municipality and the public have a duty to maintain the heritage assets and thereby aid the local tourism industry.

Source: Authors.

Environmental Sustainability and Resilience

At the start of the ADB investments, only Jaipur had some sewage collection and treatment systems. ADB's investments since 2000 have introduced systems to 26 towns. By phase 3, environmental infrastructure installed by RUIDP amounted to more than 4,000 kilometers of sewerage lines, around 20 sewage treatment plants, and more than 100 kilometers of critical drainage in flood-prone cities. This new infrastructure had two results:

- About 6 million people have been connected to a centralized sewerage system. The cities with a population density of 100 households per hectare, and that consume at least 135 liters per capita per day, were eligible for investments in sewerage systems, including treatment plants.
- More than 4 million people have been protected from prolonged urban flooding because of new stormwater drainage.

The problem of garbage has not yet been solved by RUIDP. Observers debate why that is. What is to blame: the undeveloped market for recyclables and waste, inappropriate technology, or perhaps the unavailability of land for landfills? Officials are sure that a solution for solid waste removal will be found for Rajasthan's cities, but it was not found in time to leverage ADB financing.

Still no solutions. Solid waste management remains a complicated and pervasive urban management issue throughout Rajasthan.

Sanitation and Wastewater Treatment

Since the start of the century, there was no city in Rajasthan outside of Jaipur that was collecting and treating its sewage and wastewater.[20] When ADB began investing in sewerage and wastewater systems and RUIDP began building them, local residents were not convinced that they were necessary. If they had a septic tank, this was already considered a sign of progress, as well as a substantial personal investment. If they did not have a septic tank, they probably did not have a toilet, either. So, what was the use of a sewerage system? At that time, in 2000, 66% of the population was still defecating outdoors.[21]

The ADB-financed RUIDP and the government's Clean India campaign to end open defecation are transforming the state's urban environments. The 27 largest cities in the state have either achieved substantial coverage or are in the process of providing connections to modern sewerage systems as a result of the ADB–RUIDP program. The largest cities have not yet achieved 100% coverage, but the state is providing new financing through RUIDP to help those cities reach that goal. Smaller towns need solutions suitable for their size for such problems as fecal sludge management, which RUIDP has piloted in phase 3 and will be rolling out in the secondary towns included in phase 4.

Regarding wastewater, some project cities have adopted technologies that will help them comply with the government's latest standards for the quality of treated wastewater discharges. Two plants—one in Rajsamand and the other in Bundi—employ the sequential batch reactor technology to achieve treatment levels that are within the government's upper limits. These plants require less land, and the discharged wastewater can be used in wheat production.

Fecal Sludge Management Gaining Ground

Phase 3 accomplished a major breakthrough in promoting community-wide sanitation for smaller, less dense urban areas by piloting a new fecal sludge management (FSM) approach.

Most cities and towns do not have a centralized or systematic method of collecting and disposing of sewage, unless they have benefited from sewerage investments under RUIDP. Most households rely on septic tanks, which should be emptied every 5 years. Private desludging operators dispose of sludge through natural drainage or in barren fields on the outskirts of town—legally or illegally.

FSM is a simple approach that circumvents costly sewerage systems and addresses the logistics and environmental concerns of septic tank effluent disposal. FSM endorses the use of septic tanks across the city, but recognizes that the tanks must be emptied on schedule and that the sludge must be treated according to safety standards before it is discharged into the environment.

---

[20] Note that sewage is actually a subset of wastewater. Whereas wastewater can be defined as used and dirtied water from residential and commercial sources, sewage is wastewater that has a high component of feces, urine, laundry waste, etc.

[21] World Bank. People Practicing Open Defecation (% of Population). https://data.worldbank.org/indicator/SH.STA.ODFC.ZS?year_low_desc=true.

An Operation and Maintenance Contract Salvages an Innovative, but Underperforming Sewage Treatment Plant

When Jaipur's Delawas sewage treatment plant was designed and built, there was nothing particularly innovative about it. Indeed, the plant has experienced the same problems as many other plants in Rajasthan.

The plant was built in 2006 with financing from the Rajasthan Urban Infrastructure Development Project (RUIDP), which is backed by the Asian Development Bank (ADB).

It could treat up to 125 million liters per day (MLD) of wastewater, but was receiving 130–150 MLD. So, the system was overworked and the quality of the wastewater being discharged into the drainage canals was below standard.

The operation and maintenance (O&M) of the new treatment plant was also being overstretched. The initial 5-year management contract with a private operator had lapsed, and the plant was chugging along without sufficient inputs.

One unique factor working in Delawas' favor was the staff of imaginative and determined engineers working there. As early as 2002, 3 years before the plant's completion, Dharam Raj Jangid, the superintending engineer for sewerage and drainage at RUIDP, began studying how to capture the methane gas emitted from the plant through a flare, and convert it into energy that could power the plant or be sold on the market. Water and sewage treatment plants consume costly amounts of energy, and sewage treatment plants contaminate the air with carbon dioxide (CO_2) from the methane flares they produce.

The Delawas plant needed to generate 6,000 normal cubic meters (Nm^3) of methane gas per day to convert it into enough energy to power the plant. For that, more sludge was needed than the plant was currently producing.

Jangid, who now holds a PhD in the subject, set up a laboratory at the plant and built a model reactor for testing ratios and conversions. An important research question was how to sufficiently increase the volume and thickness of sludge from the wastewater to produce a convertible gas. After many tests, he found the correct conversion rate. By adding 1% of thickened sludge from the digester mixing pump to primary sludge in the clarifier, he was able to produce 10% more sludge.

Dharam Raj Jangid, the superintendent engineer for sewerage and drainage at RUIDP, successfully developed a process to capture the methane gas that is emitted from the Delawas sewage treatment plant in Jaipur for conversion into enough energy to power the plant or for bottling the methane gas to be sold on the market.

continued on next page

The Delawas sewage treatment plant in Jaipur contracts with a private company to compress and bottle methane gas captured from the plant for sale to nearby industries. Excess bottled methane gas is bottled in 10-kilogram high-pressure cylinders and sold to nearby industries for ₹50/m³.

The methane gas was put to two uses. First, it was used as a source of electricity for on-site use. A memorandum of understanding was drafted by Jaipur Nagar Nigam, the municipal corporation responsible for providing public services to Jaipur residents. The memorandum included three parties. One of them was the Jaipur Nagar Nigam, which would guarantee the sewage treatment plant 62.5 MLD of wastewater. This was easy to do because the city was already producing twice that amount, and the plant was already receiving in excess of its 125 MLD capacity. The second party was the sewage plant operator, which ensured that the gas engine operator would receive 6,000 Nm³ of methane gas for power generation. The third party was the gas engine operator, who produced enough power from the methane gas to replace 85% of the plant's energy every year. The Delawas plant now captures the methane gas in 750-cubic meter (m³) balloons. A gas-powered alternator or generator converts the fuel into electricity for use on-site. Since 2010, Delawas has produced 300 million kilowatt-hours of on-site electricity, representing a total savings of ₹240 million.

Second, it was compressed and sold on the market. An annex of the Delawas plant also utilizes the methane gas produced. It compresses and bottles the gas for sale to nearby factories. Excess methane gas is bottled in 10-kilogram high-pressure cylinders, and sold to nearby factories for ₹50/m³. Of the total volume of gas produced, 20% is CO_2, which the sewage treatment plant removes before compressing and bottling the methane gas for sale. The captured CO_2 is used for filling fire extinguishers, which are then sold, and the balance of the CO_2 is released into on-site groves of trees. The trees purify the air.

Both uses of the methane gas have resulted in savings and revenues for the municipality, but the gas sales have turned out to be more valuable than the use of the gas on-site. They created a revenue source for the government-financed portion of the plant, which allocated some of the revenues to O&M.

A few kilometers down the road from the Delawas treatment plant, a guar gum processing factory purchases the methane gas from the Delawas plant as a safer and more efficient alternative to liquefied petroleum gas (LPG), which had been used for firing the factory's furnaces.

"Before, workers were nervous around the LPG," said Peerdan Kajla, 33, production supervisor at the Supreme Gums guar gum factory. "When an LPG tank leaks, a cloud develops on the ground around the tanks, and it's very flammable. Fortunately, we never had any accidents, but everyone is more comfortable with the methane gas."

continued on next page

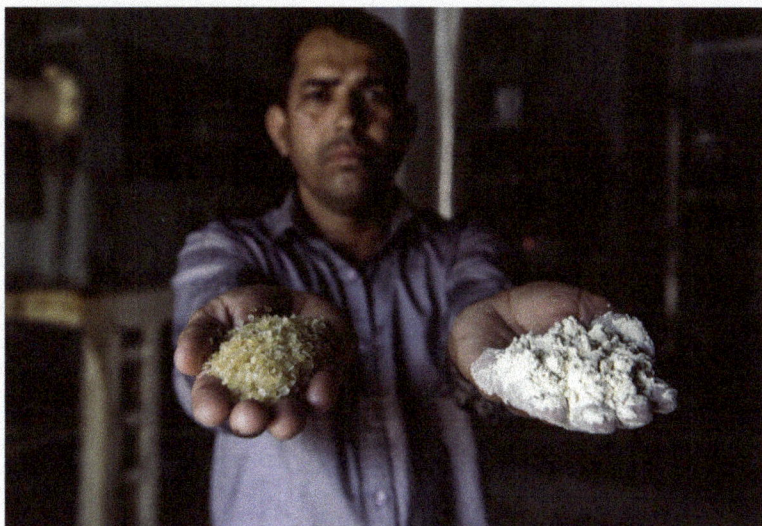

A guar gum processing factory purchases the bottled methane gas from the Delawas plant as a safer and more efficient alternative to the LPG for firing the factory's furnaces.

Mohar Estra Puni owns the guar gum factory. He had been exporting yarn and textiles before he began investing in renewable energies. Puni tried his hand at wind power for 12 years before the high competition and investment costs forced him out.

"I was looking for something new and innovative. Something I could learn from," he said. His factory uses the bottled methane to fire the furnaces that dry the guar beans before they are ground into industrial and commercial grades for exporting to the United States. Guar gum is a natural caking agent found in countless products, with a wide variety of uses, such as thickening ice cream or sealing the walls of a bore hole to enable deeper drilling for oil.

A nearby ceramics factory also purchases bottled methane from Delawas. In fact, the Delawas plant has gained international attention. "Nowhere in the world do you see these two processes side by side," Jangid said. "This is why people come here, to see and understand which process is best for their operations."

RUIDP has made power generation a mandatory design feature for sewage treatment plants built in phase 3. Construction contractors have to guarantee a minimum amount of power generation. With O&M embedded in the construction contracts, they must ensure that their system is able to produce the power.

The construction of the Delawas plant (Delawas 1), as well as the plant's O&M during its first 15 years, has also offered some lessons. Plants need to produce enough methane gas to make use of the technology possible, and they need secure O&M to produce a financially viable amount of methane gas. Another sewage treatment plant at Delawas (Delawas 2) in Jaipur has tried to replicate the Delawas 1 approach, but it could not be sustained. A sewage treatment plant in Jodhpur constructed under the Jawaharlal Nehru National Urban Renewal Mission (JNNURM) scheme is still flaring its methane gas because the volume of gas it produces is too low to be converted into energy. Jangid believes these plants' problems could be easily resolved with a small technical assistance.

continued on next page

Improvements in irrigation. Downstream farmers have installed inlets for irrigation, and have said that they have noticed improvements in their yield since the Delawas plant was built.

The Delawas plant would have produced even more methane gas for on-site energy use or for sale if the O&M contract had not collapsed and the plant had not remained without a new contract for so long afterward. Daily production dropped from the 6,000 m³ of sludge, the amount needed to fully power the plant, to just 2,000 m³ during the lean O&M years. The original management contract expired in 2011; it was extended to 2014, but with an insufficient budget for proper O&M. No new contract was awarded and signed until early 2018. From 2012 to 2017, Delawas underwent a rehabilitation, and energy production has reached 80% of its potential.

ADB and RUIDP now understand that, to prevent a costly lapse like this in the future, O&M contracts must be for longer periods, and they should ideally be signed immediately after construction. The commissioning of infrastructure building projects and initial operations involves training, observation, problem-solving, and even tariff adjustments and other reforms to cover the gaps between supply and production or the deficits that sometimes occur. Public works departments, like the Government of Rajasthan's Public Health Engineering Department, often do not have the human resources, budget, or technical capacity to take over infrastructure in less than 5 years after their commissioning. Contracts that are for 7–10 years are very effectively proving the value of extended private sector participation in the industry.

continued on next page

With management contracts becoming the norm, both the market and the Government of Rajasthan should feel more confident about making room for the private sector, for instance, in such areas as capital finance for infrastructure. The Delawas treatment plant is running beyond capacity, and Jaipur needs more treatment facilities. A $300 million public–private venture with Tata Projects has provided 175 MLD of treated wastewater, which is only enough to sustain current volumes.

The Delawas plant and the forthcoming Tata-built plants will provide downstream benefits to farmers outside the city. The treated wastewater is discharged into the Dravyavati River, which is a natural drain that varies from 30–100 meters wide and flows for 10 kilometers beyond Jaipur. The city is rehabilitating the river infrastructure. The quality of the discharged water is not good enough for drinking, but the water is viable for irrigation. So, the municipality pumps and sells 3 MLD of treated wastewater to a government colony for use in gardening.

Downstream farmers have installed inlets for irrigation, and say they have noticed improvements in their yield since the Delawas plant was built. Those farmers nearest to the Delawas plant enjoy the cleanest drainage water. However, the farther the fields are from the treatment plant, the poorer the quality of the wastewater, due to its mixing with untreated, polluted drainage. Adding to farmers' troubles are the rapidly falling groundwater tables. Farmers on the far, semi-urban outskirts of Jaipur are forced to pump water from heavily polluted drainage canals for irrigation. This illegal and a potential hazard, yet it is still done as a last resort.

A three-way relationship. The relationship among urban water supplies, drainage from urban sewage treatment plants, and semi-urban water supplies needs to be addressed in policy making and in comprehensive, integrated planning.

Source: Authors.

Overcoming an anti-technology bias. Many cities have a counterproductive bias in favor of traditional centralized sewerage systems, despite the many reasons why these systems are not a viable solution. The reasons include: the capital outlays required to build such systems, the costs of system operation and maintenance (O&M), the need to expand the system as a city grows, the risk of system failure if revenues cannot sustain O&M, and the lack of enough water supplies to keep the systems functioning at capacity.

Prior to the RUIDP investments, sewerage systems in Rajasthan did not have a good performance record. Most cities with sewerage systems in Rajasthan did not collect more than two-thirds of their wastewater, and not all of the collected wastewater was treated. The large cities treated only about two-fifths of the wastewater they generated, while the small cities with sewerage systems treated less than one-fourth.[22] O&M of such systems in the smaller towns would be even more challenging.

The advantages of FSM over traditional sewerage systems are as follows:
* It covers an entire town, not just financially viable areas.
* Construction takes 6 months, compared with 3 years for a traditional sewerage system.
* An FSM system costs $150,000–$200,000 to build, which is far less expensive than the costs of other options.
* A minimal number of employees (maximum three) are needed because the operation is biological, not mechanical.
* Electricity costs are low, as only two pumps are needed.
* Specific quantities of water, sewage, and flow are not necessary for a facility to be operational.
* O&M of the treatment facility is less demanding.
* An FSM facility will have a significantly smaller carbon footprint during its construction and operations.

Piloting fecal sludge management. Most small and medium-sized towns still require some kind of a sludge management system. Through ADB's Sanitation Financing Partnership Trust Fund, the Bill & Melinda Gates Foundation granted RUIDP $2 million for piloting more affordable, expeditious, and decentralized systems for managing urban sewage and protecting the environment. A directorate of local bodies has assessed 100 towns for the possibility of building FSM systems there, and has started preparing detailed project proposals.

To select the grant project towns, the consulting team had to be sure that a property in each town would be available for the construction of an FSM facility. It was easier to secure a "no-objection certificate" for building FSM facilities than it was to purchase land. With a no-objection certificate, the urban local body (ULB) retains ownership of the land. The project received no-objection certificates in three towns where it piloted FSM: Phulera, Khandela, and Lalsot. These three towns were chosen because they would otherwise have been unlikely to invest in a sewerage system in the next 10–15 years. All three towns are about 70–90 kilometers to the west of Jaipur.

---

[22]   World Bank. 2005. *Rajasthan Water Assessment: Status of Water Supply, Sanitation and Solid Waste Management in Urban Areas.* New Delhi: Government of India, Ministry of Urban Development, Central Public Health and Environmental Engineering Organisation (CPHEEO).

The three town councils passed resolutions that required the licensing of desludging truck operators, and the tariffs for desludging have been agreed to support the operation costs of FSM.

"People agree they want a clean city. We've done cleaning campaigns and supported the installation of toilets," said Ratan Rajora, chairperson of the Phulera Municipal Board. "We're the first municipality in Rajasthan to be open defecation-free. We are the first city to adopt FSM in Rajasthan."

The construction of all three fecal sludge treatment plants was completed in 2019. The three pilot towns now function as demonstration sites that officials from other towns can visit to learn about the best practices in FSM.

The pilots are developing comprehensive approaches to sanitation improvement that encompass long-term planning, technical innovation, institutional reforms, and financial mobilization. They also adhere to the overall approach of the World Bank's Citywide Inclusive Sanitation Initiative. The reforms are expected to streamline the entire value chain of FSM and to make progressive improvements in the overall environment, as well as in the public health indicators of all three pilot towns.

The need for a policy on fecal sludge management. RUIDP drafted a model set of regulations for municipal boards to follow when implementing FSM. Program consultants supported the publication of detailed state-level FSM guidelines on the implementation of non-sewer approaches for all the cities and towns in Rajasthan.

The draft state policy prepared under the Gates Foundation grant calls for the (i) licensing of desludging truck operators, (ii) mandatory cleaning of septic tanks every 5 years, (iii) creation of an FSM regulatory and monitoring cell at the state and local levels, and (iv) the allocation of land for fecal sludge treatment. The draft policy is pending approval by the government. In the meantime, the state government has approved *Faecal Sludge & Septic Management Guidelines for Urban Rajasthan* for use in the implementation of FSM. The guidelines, although not policy, provide practical support for FSM implementation.[23]

---

[23] Government of Rajasthan, Local Self Government Department. 2018. *Faecal Sludge & Septage Management Guidelines for Urban Rajasthan.* Jaipur. https://urban.rajasthan.gov.in/content/dam/raj/udh/organizations/ruidp/MISC/Final_State_FSSM_Guideline_upload.pdf.

The Case for Fecal Sludge Management

The advantage of the fecal sludge management (FSM) approach over traditional sewerage systems is best understood by examining its value chain. A company typically desludges a privately owned septic tank, and delivers the sludge to a municipally owned, but privately operated treatment center. The treated sludge is then mixed with organic waste to create fertilizer. An FSM treatment facility is cost-effective. It requires only few employees because the operation is biological, not mechanical; and electricity is needed for only two pumps. A standard FSM treatment facility can absorb 20 cubic meters of sewage, or 4,000 liters of sludge, per day. That is the same capacity as two to three standard sludge-hauling trucks.

Traditional sewerage systems, on the other hand, take more than 5 years to construct, are costly to construct and operate, and require a certain volume of sewage and flow. If the water supply is not adequate, a traditional sewerage system will not technically be feasible.

"FSM is not here to compete with sewage treatment plants. There is a specific market for FSM," said Suraj Kumar, the team leader for designing and implementing the FSM-related projects under the Rajasthan Urban Infrastructure Development Program (RUIDP).

The market for fecal sludge management. The market for FSM consists of the towns with fewer than 50,000 people and where septic tanks are already ubiquitous; and where the local government does not have any vested interests in the septic industry and is genuinely concerned about environmental contamination.

Inputs. For urban local bodies to recover the cost of construction and keep their FSM systems running well, they need four guarantees: a steady supply of sludge, a functioning treatment facility, the ability to charge a small user fee for treatment, and the opportunity to sell the fertilizer generated by the FSM process. If the value chain is not linked and reinforced by regulations, however, this model will fall apart.

Links in the value chain. Cities already require desludging every 5 years. The private desludging companies will not support government regulations if they do not also benefit from them. So, when contracting out for sludge collection, cities should use a licensing system for the private desludging companies, and hire only service providers that already have municipal contracts. This provides the contractors with steady revenues and enables cities to prevent environmental contamination from negligent septic tank owners and operators.

Affordability for users. The FSM model can also make septic cleaning more affordable by incorporating the desludging costs into the water bill, along with the costs of any other municipal services, for a nominal fixed fee of ₹10–₹12 per month.

"It is practically viewed as free cleaning because they don't feel the one-time higher cost, and have nothing to pay during the actual desludging operations," Kumar said.

Waste as a resource. Organic waste is needed to make fertilizer from treated sludge, specifically through composting, which entails mixing organic food waste with soil or sludge to further process and dry the sludge. The resulting mix is usable fertilizer, so it can be sold or given to farmers as an agricultural input. Organic waste can be easily collected from vegetable markets and agricultural fields. However, an FSM plan also provides an opportunity to work out a system for encouraging or imposing recycling, including the separation of kitchen scraps and recyclable materials (plastic, cardboard, glass, tin, etc.) from household garbage. City administrators and urban planners in many Indian states and cities have never managed to enforce a requirement to separate recyclable materials at the household level. If just 30% of a town practiced household separation, the waste-to-resource model could be sustained.

continued on next page

A better way to dispose of waste.
Rather than disposing septic tank effluents into natural drainage sites or barren fields on the outskirts of towns—legally or illegally—the FSM approach includes greater regulation and environmental protection. Licensed private operators become contractors for the city and the plants, ensuring a more sustainable system for all stakeholders.

Source: Authors.

Drainage and Flood Protection

When it rains, it floods in many of Rajasthan's arid cities.

A number of factors cause the flooding. Certainly, the lack of a proper drainage system is high on the list of factors, but unplanned and uncontrolled development, depressions in the ground due to the overextraction of groundwater, and the impervious surfaces of concretized earth have all added to the problems during the monsoon season and occasional rain bursts at other times.

ADB investments in drainage systems are creating flow where there used to be floodwaters that stood for hours, or even days, in the middle of the busiest city crossroads. A municipality that can recover from storms quickly will be especially competitive when it comes to attracting industries. Drains keep the economy moving during the monsoon season, and protects people from the health and safety hazards of traveling through deep and dirty floodwaters to reach home, work, or school. Drainage also protects property and assets.

Impact Story 21

New Pumps Keep Churu's Bowl-Like Terrain Free of Flooding

The city of Churu is the first place that engineers working for the Rajasthan Urban Infrastructure Development Project (RUIDP) will mention when they talk about urban floods. Churu used to experience about 25 days of flooding every year in different parts of the city.

Whenever you mention "1992" to Purnmal Saine, the 55-year-old owner of Amit Building Materials and Tent House, in Churu, his eyes widen and he says, "Ohhhhhh," and he starts to rub his knees as if the mere mention of that very wet year brought back aches to his joints. "That year, there were 6 hours of rain every day for as many days as he could remember," he said. Saine once had to stay in his shop for a week until the floods subsided. He recounted how there would be flooding in the streets of 2–3 feet as often as 10 times a year. The floodwaters would typically take at least a day to recede.

Down the road from Purnmal Saine's shop, Jagadish Fulcrum Saine, 40, who has been driving an auto rickshaw in this flood-prone part of the city since the late 1990s, recalled floods that did not recede for a month. It was not possible for people to commute using his auto rickshaw. He came to expect these floods year after year, knowing that he would earn about a third less during the monsoons. "The kids, the students, they would take the bus and use other routes then. But now there is no waterlogging at all." He knew it was because RUIDP had done its work.

Krishna Kumar Saine is a young man who owns a tea shop that often serves the local auto rickshaw drivers. His family rents a flat within a few steps of his shop, on a street that was notorious for its flooding. He has lived in this area for most of this life. It is where he can earn a living and afford a home. So, during the monsoons, he and his family struggled. "We would try to bail the water out of the house when it rained. It would work for smaller rains, but not the big ones," he said. "We were not afraid because we knew the floods would come. The problem was when the rain came at night."

continued on next page

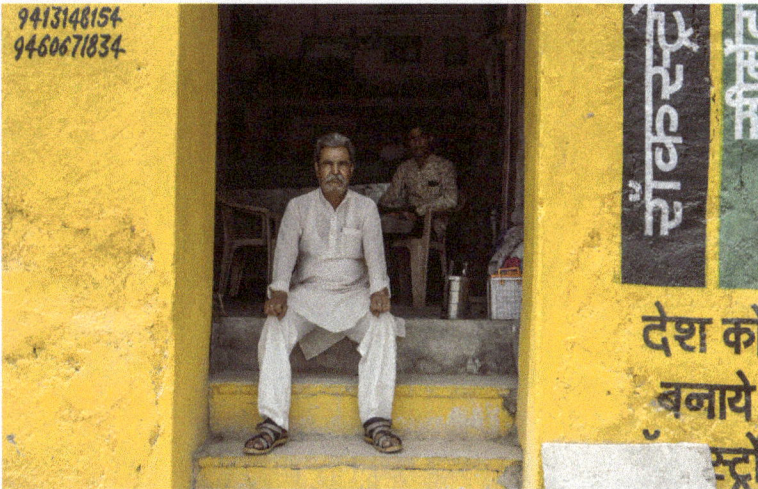

"A long time ago, waterlogging used to happen, but there were no roads, no construction, so the water used to go into the ground very quickly ... After the construction of the pump house, the flooding went down."

Trapped by the floods. Purnmal Saine would often get trapped inside his tent rental and building supply shop during the rains of the monsoon season.

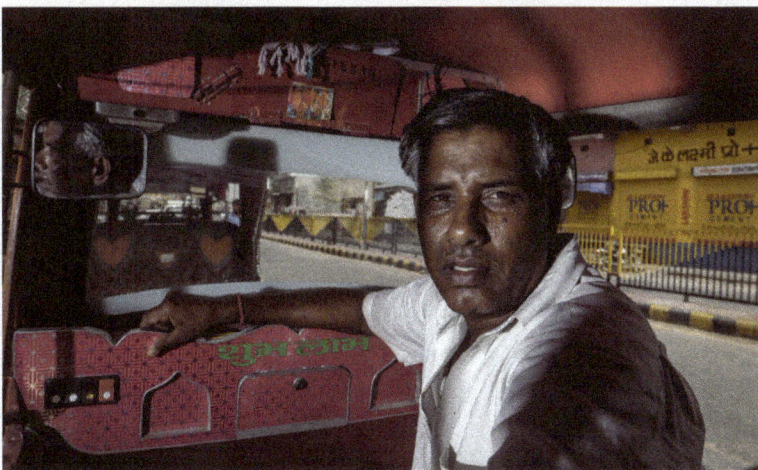

"The kids, the students, they would take the bus and use other routes then. But now there is no waterlogging at all."

More flooding, less income. Jagadish Fulcrum Saine, an auto rickshaw driver, knew that that his income would drop by a third during the monsoon season.

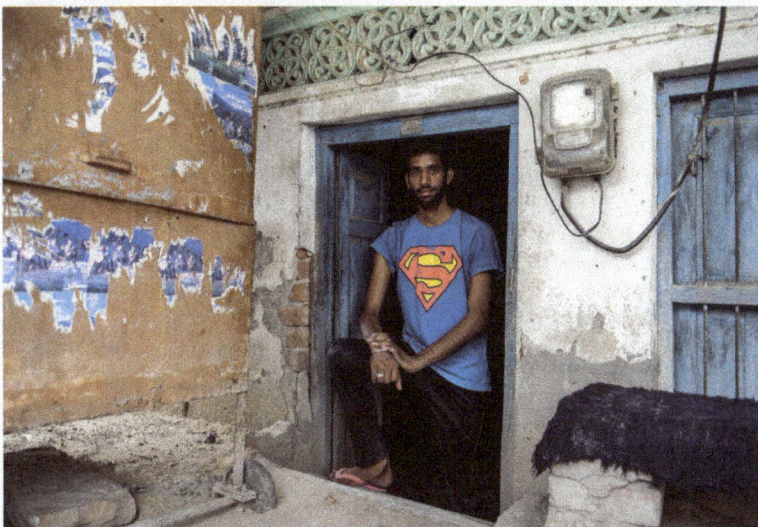

"We just struggled. We would try to bail the water out of the house when it rained. It would work for smaller rains, but not the big ones..."

When the floods hit home. Krishna Kumar Saine, who owns a tea shop, lives with his family on a street that was notorious for its flooding.

continued on next page

Churu's bowl-like terrain. As the topography of Churu resembles a bowl, the floodwater would rush in and collect in two particularly low-lying areas of the city. RUIDP installed two pumps (one of them pictured above) to reduce flooding in those areas.

People describe Churu's topography as resembling a bowl. The floodwaters would rush in and collect in two particularly low-lying areas. RUIDP has installed two pumps to reduce the flooding in those areas.

Purnmal Saine has another theory, which is also correct: "A long time ago, waterlogging used to happen, but there were no roads, no construction, so the water used to go into the ground very quickly," he said. He was talking about a problem many cities have due to the loss of natural surfaces that could quickly absorb the rainwater and allow it to drain into the groundwater aquifers. Today, cities like Churu are essentially concrete blankets over the land, so water rushes around without finding a place to drain.

"I still have bags of cement that were ruined by floods. I haven't been able to move them yet," he said. But now they are reminders of all that's changed—for the better. "After the construction of the pump house, the flooding went down."

A planned new sewerage system will also relieve the accumulation of wastewater. The city currently relies on combined wastewater and stormwater drains. About 65% of the city's wastewater still flows into the stormwater drains.

Source: Authors.

Controlling Floodwater Flows in Kota

In the city of Kota, the Rajasthan Urban Infrastructure Development Project (RUIDP) succeeded in diverting rainwater runoff that used to rush into the city center, driving residents to the upper floors of their homes and offices, where they would sometimes have to wait for days until the floodwaters receded.

"Even the normal rains would mean floods were coming," said longtime resident P.L. Sharma, 78. "People were prepared for the rains, though. They would keep stones and bricks to stack their things on, and they would watch for the floods because they would come with force."

There were some particularly memorable floods, like the one in 1987. Sharma vividly remembers when the water level rose so high, it broke the barrage walls outside the community and cars floated away.

Residents in the flood-prone parts of Kota recall 3–4 feet of floodwaters carrying along broken walls, floating cars, and even snakes. Factories would have to close due to the flooding, and water lines would break.

"People would come here to see the floods for their amusement. We were an exhibition," said Hari Om Gupta, 52, a juice vendor and convenience shop owner in Vigyan Nagar Colony, a neighborhood in Kota city. "There were floods for 2 kilometers in every direction from this place." Gupta would lose at least 2 days of work, but he sold his fruit from a mobile cart, so he could transfer any section of the city that was dry and passable. He would not have dared open a shop where he now has one. But since the Asian Development Bank (ADB) invested in flood protection and drainage projects in Kota, implemented by RUIDP, waterlogged streets have no longer been a threat, and Gupta felt safe enough to invest in permanent prime real estate to set up a fruit shop.

Flooding as a perennial problem. "Even the normal rains would mean floods were coming," said longtime Kota resident P. L. Sharma. "People were prepared for the rains, though."

Making Kota safe for business. Since ADB invested in flood protection and drainage in Kota, waterlogged streets are no longer a threat, and a local fruit vendor, Hari Om Gupta, has felt safe enough to invest in permanent prime real estate to set up a shop.

Source: Authors.

Equity and Inclusion

As much as urban development is about making cities more productive and efficient, it should also be about lightening the burden of people's poverty and creating greater chances for the city's poor. Cities have always attracted the poor from the countryside, but they have never provided them with housing or connections to urban services. The deprived millions living in Rajasthan's slums are a vital part of the urban labor force, and they are slowly gaining the recognition and resources they deserve from infrastructure investments.

The ADB–RUIDP investments are often implemented first in low-income communities, where they are most needed. The provision of more water supplies, now on a 24/7 basis, and of connections to sewerage systems, is transforming communities and inspiring self-determined development. The water supply, sanitation, and drainage infrastructure has also enabled communities to take advantage of national housing and sanitation development programs. New and upgraded public hospitals have brought affordable quality health care and more dignified hospital experiences within reach of the cities and their hinterlands, especially for the poor, who tended to find health services inaccessible.

A socioeconomic survey conducted for the program's appraisal for phase 1 found that about 50% of the intended beneficiaries were poor and about 19% lived in extreme poverty. The poor have suffered in particular from inadequate and unsafe water supplies and sanitation. In 2000, of the women and children in the project areas, 30% needed to fetch water every day. The ADB–RUIDP interventions would eliminate their daily trips to pumps or wells, thus providing them with time for more personal pursuits.

The program was expected to improve living conditions and make many people healthier. Before RUIDP was initiated, there had been a higher prevalence of vector-borne diseases in Rajasthan than in the rest of India. For instance, 5,103 cases of malaria per 100,000 residents were reported in 1992–1993, compared with an average of 3,324 cases per 100,000 in the country as a whole. Better water supplies and sanitation services would eventually reduce exposure to pathogens, and especially benefit children, who were the most susceptible to waterborne diseases.

Phase 1 proved to be transformative, though not at the intended scale. The program expected to improve 220 slums, benefiting 600,000 people, but investments were only possible in 129 slums, and reached only 100,000 people. Some cities, especially Udaipur, were reluctant to borrow funds for the interventions; other cities ran behind schedule, so they dropped key social programs that would have helped the poor, such as thrift and credit societies and community centers.

A survey of project benefits found that the average monthly household income in the affected slums increased by 80%–95%. Slum households had also invested in housing in the wake of the project. The number of houses built with makeshift or temporary material had decreased by 76%, which indicated that the living standards of slum dwellers had improved.

Some of the RUIDP plans for slum upgrading were picked up by ADB's Japan Fund for Poverty Reduction (JFPR), which then exceeded the plans' targets significantly. The program benefited 25,000 slum families through improvements in the environment and in the quality of life due to better drainage, sanitation, toilets, garbage collection, and awareness campaigns. The target had been 20,000 families, but a total of 5,000 families ended up benefiting from access to drinking water through rainwater harvesting, 2,000 more than envisaged. The JFPR component also benefited 2,000 families by employing family members as garbage collectors, thereby achieving its employment target. A particularly successful intervention was the introduction of a computer education program in low-income areas, using mobile buses as classrooms. The state's education department offices in three project cities—Jaipur, Jodhpur, and Bikaner—had proposed the idea.

Phase 2 investments in slums has doubled the beneficiary population to 210,000 people. Phase 3 has mainstreamed slum development into the program's design. Slums were given priority during the implementation of total coverage systems for water supplies, sewerage, and drainage.

More water to come. Mahadewali, a slum in the town of Tonk, is scheduled to receive a 24/7 water supply system under phase 3 of RUIDP.

A Slum Upgrading in Jodhpur during the Early Program Years Transformed Properties, Expectations

The Rajasthan Urban Infrastructure Development Project (RUIDP) upgraded nearly 60 slums in Jodhpur during phase 1 with investments from the Asian Development Bank (ADB), benefiting nearly 25% of households in the city.

To connect the poor to public services, RUIDP worked with the state's Public Health Engineering Department to revise existing policies. The result: for the first time, affected households received running water, a connection to the sewerage system, and drainage services. Newly paved roads and installed street lights brought more security and mobility. The idea of 24/7 water supplies was not yet imagined during phase 1. During that phase, slums received official connections that typically provided them with 1.5–2 hours of water per day.

With more livable conditions, residents began to realize the value of the land they had acquired from the government as part of the process. Some families sold their properties. Others stayed and upgraded their homes, replacing temporary materials with sturdier permanent ones, and now these communities are unrecognizable from the time when they were slums.

Nat Basti Masuriya, in Jodhpur's Maderna Colony, was one of the first slums to be upgraded by RUIDP with ADB investments in water supply, sewerage, and drainage infrastructure. It has remained a slum, but the community is much better off than what it would have been without the investments. One problem is that the community's location in a low-catchment area and the lack of competent solid waste management has diminished the impact of the drainage system that RUIDP built.

Families in Nat Basti Masuriya say they have lived there for seven generations. There was a time "when this was a forest and we were far from Jodhpur, and nobody came here and bothered us," according to resident Ramesh Kumar Raj Nat. Due to its name, which means to perform plays, and the occasional performances at festivals, the community is known for its main source of income: child acrobats.

ADB's investments in Nat Basti Masuriya and other slums have helped to integrate them into the city because they connected these communities to official systems, making the residents customers of Jodhpur city services.

Much achieved, but more to do.
"Yes, our community has changed," said Ramesh Kumar Raj Nat, a resident of Nat Basti Masuriya, in reference to the effects of earlier RUIDP investments. "If I think how my father lived, our lives are 50% better." But, he added, "we still have many problems. This is not the life we want."

continued on next page

Some residents recalled the work done by RUIDP from 2003 to 2005. "I remember the name of the man from RUIDP who used to come here," said Nat. His father was the community leader who signed the agreement with RUIDP signifying the community's support. A condition of their support was a 500-meter paved road leading to the construction site. That road looks very different now, having lived well beyond its expected lifetime of just 5 years.

"Yes, our community has changed," he said. "The children here used to work, entertaining people, dancing, acrobatics. Now, look at them: They are in school. But we still have many problems. This is not the life we want. We just continue to live life. I think of how my father lived, and I believe our lives are 50% better than his."

Slums in cities like Jodhpur are prime candidates for reinvestment, especially for the provision of water 24/7. The impact of the initial investments has eroded, and the infrastructure that was built at the time is showing signs of neglect. But the residents now have even higher expectations. Infrastructure does not only change the environment and the way people go about their daily routines. It also changes the way people think. Infrastructure makes people want more and more. For some things, like the quality of their housing, they want and expect more from themselves. For other things, communal things like the maintenance of parks and roads, the provision of electricity, flood control, and garbage collection, they want and expect more from the government.

Children performing academically. Once born to be child acrobats as a means of livelihood for their families, the children of the Nat Basti Masuriya slum now attend school. Some still perform, but only during festivals. This was one of the first low-income communities to be upgraded by RUIDP.

Source: Authors.

Hospitals

In 2003, 4 years into the first phase of ADB investments in Rajasthan's cities, the program had accrued savings, and some of those funds were reallocated to the upgrade of a total of 17 health facilities in Jaipur, Ajmer, Kota, and Udaipur. The hospital subprojects comprised 3% of the total phase 1 program costs, but they had a catalytic effect that is still reverberating through the hospitals' halls over 15 years later. The benefit monitoring reports noted that hospitals had improved their capacity to serve, as well as the quality of their facilities and services. According to the report, the numbers of admissions and outpatients had increased by an average of 21%, and overall hospital facilities had improved. Specifically, there had been

- a 50% reduction in the average waiting time for emergency cases;
- a 33% increase in the number of cases attended to per day;
- a reduction in the average time taken to attend to emergencies, from 15 minutes (pre-project) to 5 minutes (post-project);
- a 30% overall improvement in cleanliness; and
- improvements in more patient waiting rooms in the hospitals.

The addition of laundry facilities and industrial equipment was a small investment with a huge impact, especially for hospital workers who must launder soiled linens all day.

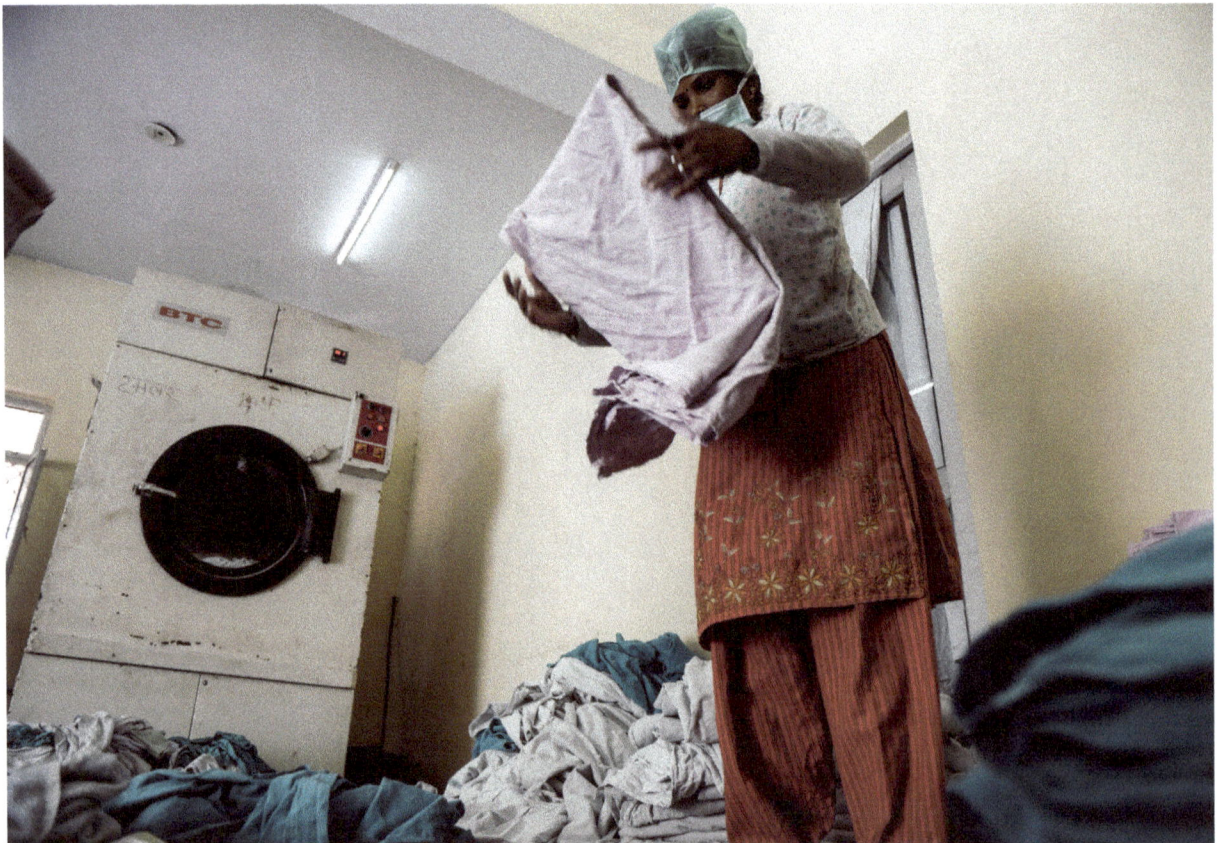

More professional laundry facilities. JK Lon Hospital and four other hospitals in Rajasthan now use industrial laundry equipment financed by the ADB–RUIDP project.

Hospital Construction and Renovations Catalyze Expansion of Care

A Children's Hospital in Jaipur

At the JK Lone Mother and Child Hospital in Jaipur, which specializes in pediatrics, investments from the Asian Development Bank (ADB) were catalytic. They funded the creation of modern spaces that made admissions more orderly and outpatient waiting more comfortable. Private long-term space was added for families of intensive care patients. Operating rooms were constructed, and the number of surgery-related cases increased by 10%. Emergency cases were 29% higher after the program investments. The funding also supported the purchase of machines for more hygienic laundry services. These improvements funded by ADB were implemented by the Rajasthan Urban Infrastructure Development Program (RUIDP).

Medical doctor and hospital superintendent Ashok Gupta, 58, said that the upgrades had shown the board and management what could be achieved, and they responded by taking on even more capital investments. As a result, a courtyard that had been used for collecting waste was converted into a covered indoor playground area, with artificial grass and natural lighting, so it can be open all year.

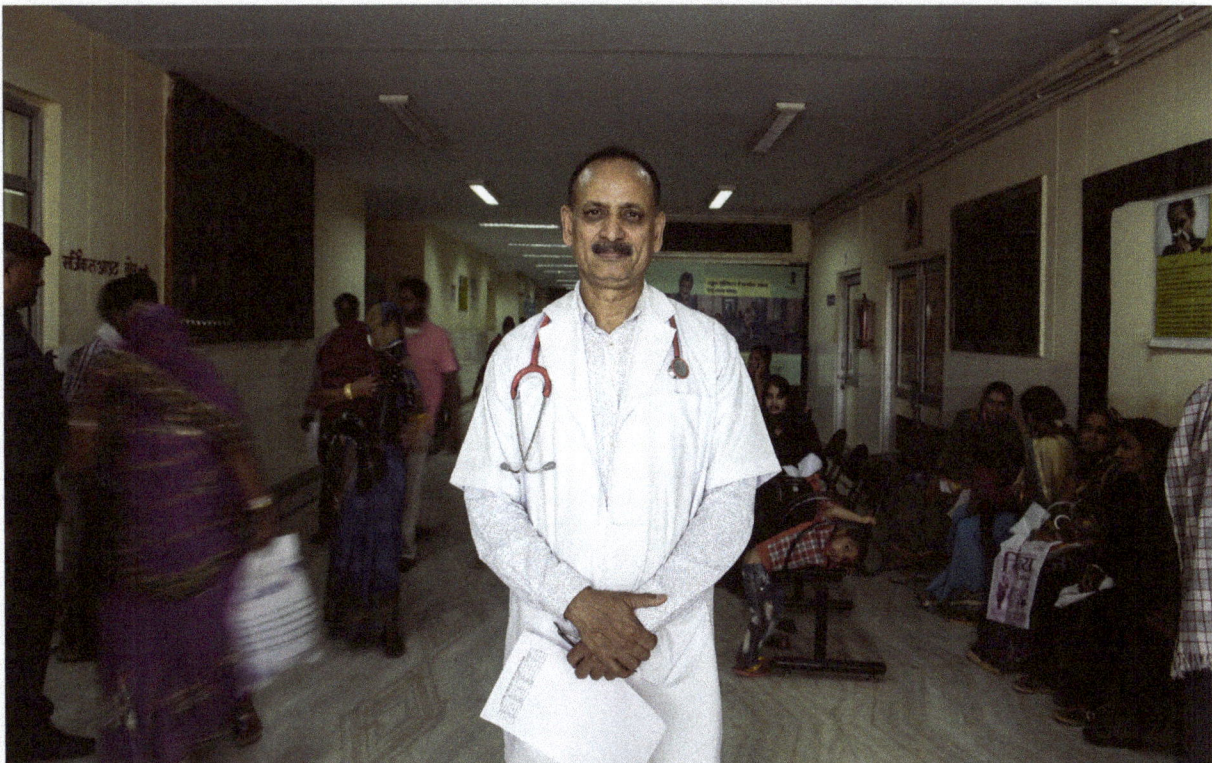

Better facilities, better morale. Ashok Gupta, medical doctor and superintendent of JK Lone Mother and Child Hospital, in Jaipur, which specializes in pediatrics, said that ADB's investments showed the hospital board and management what could be achieved, and they responded by taking on even more capital investments. Gupta believes that the improvements in the hospital facilities have helped to retain staff and generate more pride in the institution.

continued on next page

"The light and the air flow throughout the hospital helps patients recover faster,"

Ashok Gupta, medical doctor and superintendent of JK Lone Mother and Child Hospital, in Jaipur

"The light and the air flow throughout the hospital helps patients recover faster," he said.

Gupta also believes that the improvements in the hospital facilities have helped to retain staff and generate more pride in the institution. The hospital employs 270 doctors and 400 nurses. When staff talk about the hospital, they often refer to the work "we do," rarely referring to their personal work. It indicates a sense of belonging and loyalty, and a desire to be identified with the place and the group of professionals working there.

The hospital treats 500,000 babies every year and has 960 beds for pediatric patients. One-third of the patients are not residents of Rajasthan, but travel there for the specialized medical care.

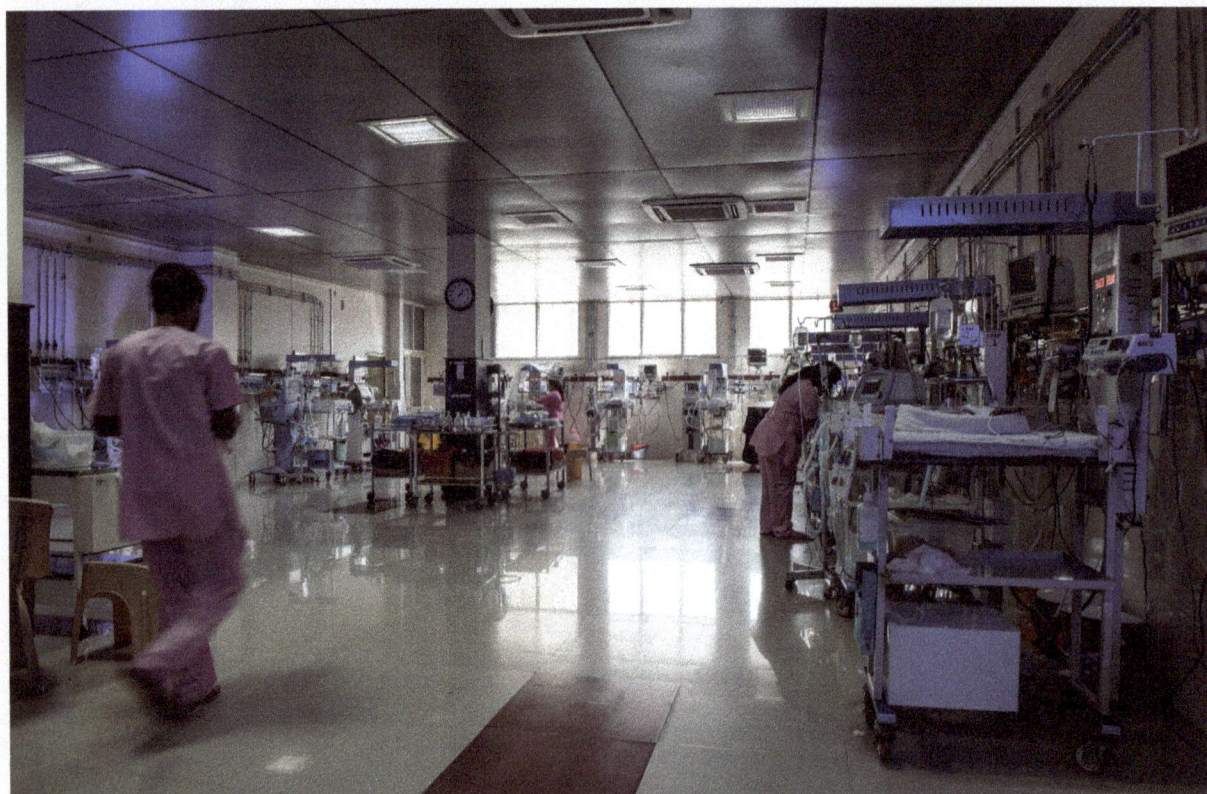

A new ward. The pediatric intensive care ward at JK Lon Hospital, pictured here, was built with funding from the ADB–RUIDP investment program.

continued on next page

Better facilities, better comfort. Pulli Devi (left) said that she appreciated the comfortable private waiting rooms for the families of patients at JK Lon Hospital. She had traveled 12 hours to get there with her pregnant daughter-in-law, who gave birth prematurely.

Pulli Devi, 60, brought her pregnant daughter-in-law to JK Lon Hospital after their obstetrician in their hometown of Fatehpur (a 4-hour drive to Jaipur) referred her to a hospital in Sikar district, in Rajasthan (a 2-hour drive). The doctors there referred her to JK Lon Hospital for treatment of complications, and that is where her daughter-in-law gave birth prematurely, with the baby remaining in the intensive care unit for 6 days.

"I am just grateful that both my daughter-in-law and her child could be saved. This was her first child," said Devi. "Because other hospitals sent us here, we know it is better. My grandson was saved, so this hospital is good enough for me." Gupta is hoping to raise funds to build a more convenient and hygienic food court for the patients' families and hospital staff.

> "I am just grateful that both my daughter-in-law and her child could be saved. This was her first child...
> Because other hospitals sent us here, we know it is better.
> My grandson was saved, so this hospital is good enough for me."

Pulli Devi, 60

continued on next page

Witnessing a hospital's growth. Meena Damor, medical doctor, began working at Chandpol Hospital, in Udaipur, in 2005. At the time, it was a simple clinic and dispensary. In 2009, RUIDP built the current facility with ADB funding, and launched it as a satellite hospital. During her tenure, the satellite hospital also developed into a district hospital, as well as a clinical training facility for a medical school.

From Dispensary to District Hospital in Udaipur

Medical doctor Meena Damor, 54, began working at Udaipur's Chandpol Hospital in 2005, when it was a simple clinic and dispensary. It barely had a roof over its operations.

In 2009, ADB–RUIDP investments funded the construction of the current facility, which launched it as a satellite hospital. During her tenure, the satellite hospital also developed into a district hospital, as well as a clinical training facility for a medical school. Damor is now the principal specialist in pediatrics and deputy director of the Chandpol Satellite District Hospital.

"The building was the catalyst for it all," she said, sitting at a desk that was likely shared by several administrators. Damor wore a stethoscope draped around her shoulders and a hygiene mask around her neck. She had to shift back and forth between her administrative duties and the long line of patients waiting outside her office. "The building helped me do my job better. But we could do with even more space. We have a great problem again with congestion."

continued on next page

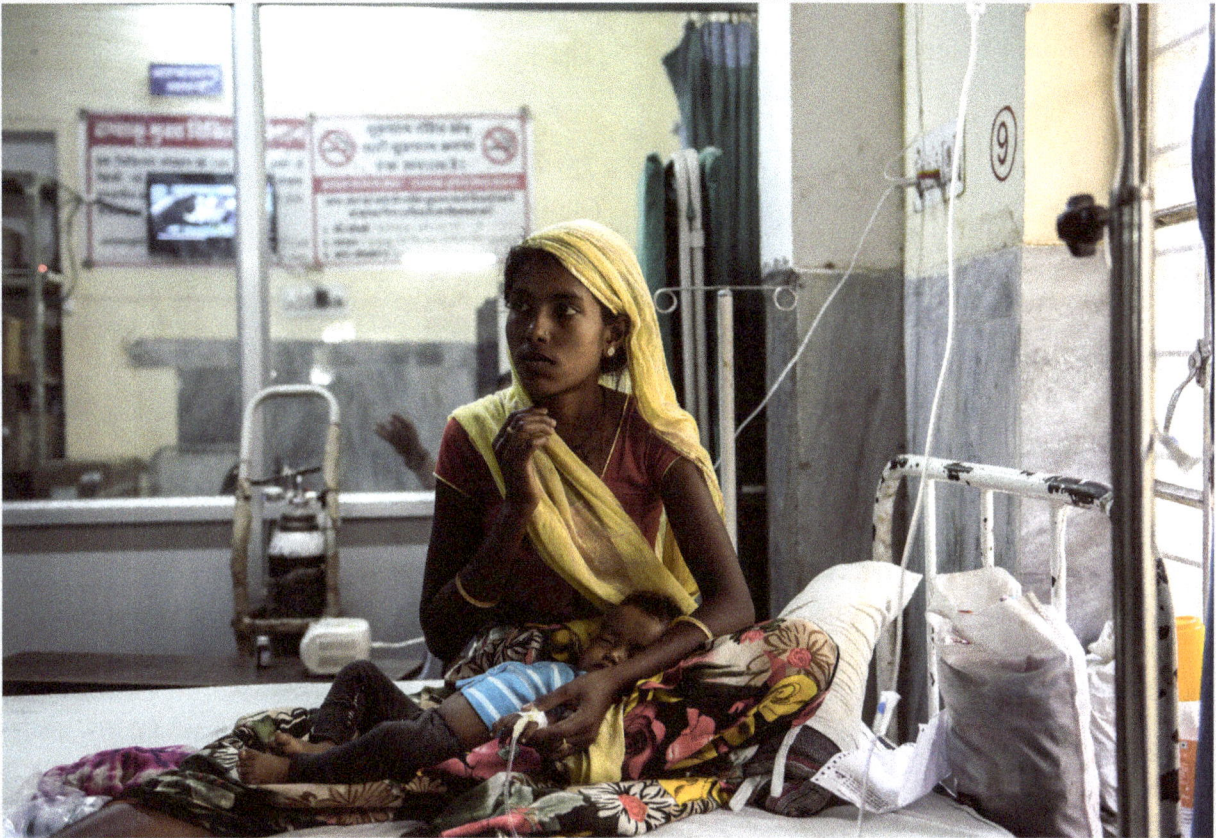

A route to recovery. Lata, 27, traveled 25 kilometers from Rudali village in Uttar Pradesh, to Chandpol Satellite District Hospital to get treatment for her daughter's fever. The hospital was built by RUIDP with ADB investments. It is the first stop for people in remote areas seeking diagnosis and treatment.

When the clinic was upgraded to a satellite hospital and then a district hospital, it gave the administration access to more resources. "There was no trust before because nothing existed. We had nothing to show for our work."

Today, the hospital has five times the outpatient flow, with increases both in the number of hospital births and operations. "The building also gave us access to the people," she added. "This is where the poor can come and get fair access to treatment." It is the first stop for patients coming from remote areas, when they receive an initial diagnosis and treatment. "We treat this hospital like a temple," said Damor. "People are looking for help. We empathize with them. We can help. We do our best to treat them. We don't treat people half-heartedly. They don't have to go to private hospitals or private doctors."

The hospital is open 24/7, and the staff members go out on house calls and do door-to-door consultations in the city and the outskirts.

Source: Authors.

Fire Safety

Compared with the capital expenditures on major infrastructure projects, the ADB–RUIDP investments in firefighting were relatively small, but they addressed the growing risk of fires in urban areas. ADB financed the construction of 14 fire stations, mainly in Rajasthan's largest cities; the procurement of vehicles and equipment; and the training of new firefighters and medics.

Chittorgarh was one of the few smaller cities to invest ADB funds in its fire brigade. It had one fire station, but half the city was cut off from that station when the trains came through town, causing the railroad crossings to close to let them pass. The crossings were closed as much as 6 hours a day, given that up to 35 trains passed through the city every day. The municipal corporation owned an ideal site for a new fire station, and now that station gets about 10–15 emergency calls every week, 90% of them fire-related.

RUIDP surveyed three of the six large cities receiving phase 1 investments to measure the benefits of the new fire stations funded by those investments. The survey found that the sampled fire stations in Jaipur and Jodhpur responded to fire emergencies 33% faster than they had before the project investments.

The benefits survey also found that residents were generally not willing to pay for fire services directly, believing that the municipal government should provide the services for free. But public opinion may be changing. Demand for more municipal fire stations and trucks is reportedly growing, and state funds are being released to improve fire and emergency services. *The Times of India* reported in 2018 that 90 municipalities in Rajasthan (40% of the total) did not have fire stations, and that 53 cities did not have either a fire station or even just a fire truck.[24] Some cities relied on the services of other cities 25 kilometers away. The media have also exposed the need for a systematic approach to firefighting in the cities.[25] Fire departments need fire safety laws, regulations, and plans. They need to know more about a city's outlay and activities, for instance, where industries are using and keeping inventories of hazardous materials and the status of no-objection certificates for the electrical work on construction projects. Until adequate legal and administrative systems are in place, along with the provision of more fire stations, equipment, and trained personnel, cities will remain exposed to the threat of fire. The municipal governments' acknowledgment of these gaps would be a first step toward the better protection of urban citizens from fire.

Enabling Environment

Infrastructure-centric investment programs require the support of competent institutions, strong governance, and a high professional capacity of the people involved. These are all necessary for prolonging the lifetime of the assets and ensuring that their impact is achieved and sustained in the form of service delivery to the public. This trifecta of strong institutions, governance, and capacity is especially important for the process of decentralization. Assets and service responsibilities cannot be turned over by the state to

---

24   *The Times of India.* 2018. 90 Municipalities across Rajasthan Don't Have Fire Stations. 15 January. https://timesofindia .indiatimes.com/city/jaipur/90-municipalities-across-state-dont-have-fire-stations/articleshow/62501360.cms.

25   *Hindustan Times.* 2018. Decoding the Flames: Why is Jaipur Burning? 15 April. https://www.hindustantimes.com/jaipur/ decoding-the-flames-why-is-jaipur-burning/story-zJzZj4EpJ5mi6H6Kfx8ZZN.html.

urban local bodies (ULBs) unless accompanied by guidance in the form of policies, financing in the form of revenue streams, and knowledge in the form of capacity-building programs. Without these supports, the infrastructure will fail due to the lack of leadership, financing, and knowledge that is required to guarantee the adequate operation and maintenance (O&M) of assets and services.

Since 2000, many states in India have pursued urban policy reforms of differing scales, sizes, and nature—but rarely as comprehensively as has Rajasthan. For example, Maharashtra and Gujarat have focused on policy reforms targeting water supplies and sanitation; while Tamil Nadu and Andhra Pradesh have focused on solid waste, sewerage, and public–private partnerships. Other states have taken up new policies on urban transport, housing, and property taxes. In most states, however, the reforms rely heavily on the ULBs, with the state governments providing only general policy direction and some funding.

ADB provided Rajasthan with the financial stimulus for a comprehensive urban reform agenda that included support at the state policy-making level and at the ULB implementation level. As part of phase 3, which officially began in late 2015, ADB has financed a $250 million loan to support the state government's efforts to achieve 10 policy objectives that it had begun pursuing in late 2013, during phase 2, aimed at strengthening the state's institutions, urban governance, and capacity.[26] The Rajasthan government received its first of the two installments in 2015 and the second in 2019, each installment coming after achieving the policy objectives.

Rajasthan's reform agenda is specific and measurable, and it empowers the ULBs with a clear delegation of functions, as well as the financial resources and autonomy necessary to implement policies through locally appropriate strategies. Using ADB's reform stimulus, the state government provides ULBs with administrative, managerial, and technical support. One way it does this is through a recently established training institute that offers capacity-building courses in urban development tailored to the unique local issues and training needs of each ULB and stakeholder group.

The program's loan disbursements, in the form of reimbursements to the state for the resources spent on the reforms, could have been legally absorbed into the state's general funding. However, successful policy dialogues involving ADB, the state government, and RUIDP led to an agreement to reallocate all program loan disbursements to RUIDP as capital. With these disbursements, RUIDP expanded the scope of the phase 3 infrastructure-focused project loan to include seven more cities.

---

[26] ADB, RUIDP. 2014. *Economic Analysis: Program Loan.* Manila. This document includes the following: "The amount of the program loan is based on the development financing needs and the costs of reforms, which, among others, would include support for (i) capitalization of the corporatized state-level institution for urban development and the corporatized water and sewerage utility for Jaipur—about $25 million; (ii) implementation of urban development policy and human resource development plan, including setting up a training institute of urban governance—about $25 million; (iii) delegation of water supply operations to municipal bodies with adequate personnel and O&M budget—about $75 million; (iv) implementation of nonrevenue water assessment and reduction and operationalization of 24-hour supply in the state—about $50 million; (v) implementation of other items in the urban water and sanitation … about $75 million."

This section summarizes the policy objectives supported by the program loan. Many policy objectives were achieved in 2019, and are at a nascent stage, requiring more years of support and monitoring to further their impacts. In some cases, the state government exceeded the required achievement target, showing ownership and commitment to the reforms. Phase 4 will continue to support the implementation and monitoring of state government reforms, evolution of new urban institutions, and capacity building.

Reforms to Strengthen Urban Institutions

Four of RUIDP's policy objectives focused on strengthening public institutions. At a statewide level, the Government of Rajasthan created an umbrella corporation for urban development projects in order to solidify RUIDP's presence in the urban sector. The state capital, Jaipur, established a corporate water utility that consolidated the roles and responsibilities of the relevant public and private agencies and improved coordination. The state government also piloted the decentralization of the water supply and sewerage utilities in RUIDP's phase 3 project cities. As a way of monitoring and evaluating the progress of the water utilities, the program loan has supported the establishment of performance baselines and benchmarks, which also help to identify where investments are needed and to make a case for those cities seeking additional project financing.

Establishment of a Corporatized, State-Level Organization for Urban Development

Issue. Rajasthan's cities are fragmented, so they need a unifying, vibrant, and autonomous institution to provide technical and financial assistance with urban development, especially for small and medium-sized ULBs that fall outside the state government's budget and do not meet lending criteria.

Solution. Given RUIDP's many years of demonstrated success, the state government already had a model for such an institution, one that could generate similarly positive results for urban water supplies, sewerage and wastewater, housing, and other urban services. So, in 2015, the state government established the Rajasthan Urban Drinking Water, Sewerage & Infrastructure Corporation (RUDSICO) as an umbrella urban development corporation that would support the municipalities.

The members of RUDSICO's board of directors are high-level state government officials, including Rajasthan's minister of local self government (as chair), RUDSICO's executive director, and the RUIDP project director.

RUDSICO is the operational mechanism for implementing urban-related policies and reforms throughout the state. As such, it is responsible for the following core operational functions:
- supporting municipalities' project management, especially with national urban program funding and overseas development assistance;
- providing ULBs with financial support and consultancy services (e.g., technical, financial);
- conducting surveys for schemes and programs relating to infrastructure development;
- distributing, on behalf of the state government, grants in aid and financial assistance to ULBs;
- arranging or raising funds from public agencies, institutional investors, and banks or other financial institutions; and
- planning and financially monitoring all types of projects related to the development of urban areas in Rajasthan.

Results. RUDSICO is managing projects in more than 60 cities that are financed by the central government, state government, or ADB. Following in the footsteps of RUIDP, RUDSICO aspires to be a top-rated professional organization in the field of urban development in India, and its policies provide a good model for other states.

The board has adopted a detailed business plan (covering the short, medium, and long terms) that details RUDSICO's business strategy, mission, vision, objectives, functions, and operational modalities. The Human Resource Development Policy details the organizational structure, staffing, and any human resource practices to be followed.[27] In keeping with RUIDP's autonomous nature, the Human Resource Development Policy calls for the independent recruitment of employees by means of absorption from state government departments, external market hiring, and campus recruitment. The consolidation of the various urban entities into RUDSICO has involved the challenge of integrating traditional systems, practices, and decision-making protocols. Harmonizing them and developing RUDSICO's corporate governance will be a focus of the phase 4 investments.

The program loan has also supported the establishment of a technical design center, as well as a social safeguards unit and a gender equality unit within RUDSICO. The units are staffed by RUDSICO permanent employees and consultants working as advisors, managers, and field implementers. The units help prepare frameworks during the design phase of projects, and they have teams to implement and monitor the frameworks throughout the project cycle. The units are already supporting more than 35 cities in line with the central government's Atal Mission for Rejuvenation and Urban Transformation (AMRUT) and various infrastructure projects supported by the state government. For project-specific work, a social safeguards unit oversees the environmental, gender, social development, communications, and participation aspects.

Impact Story 25

New Social Safeguards Unit Reflects Historical Needs, Potential of Women in Rajasthan

Before the 1980s, the Thar Desert town of Jaisalmer relied on a rain-fed lake and a few wells for its water supply. The lake was as volatile, as can be expected under desert conditions. People here remember the time when there was only enough water to bathe once a week, and they washed their hands with ghee.

Kavita Kailash Khatri, chair of the Jaisalmer Municipal Council, remembers coming to Jaisalmer as a young bride in 1981. She is from a water-rich district in nearby Jodhpur. "Before coming here, I had never put an earthen pot on my head," she said. "Jaisalmer was like a culture shock for me. Nobody liked this job of carrying water, but we had to do it to keep the household going. We had no choice." There were 15 members in her household, and the women spent up to 3 hours every day collecting water.

continued on next page

---

27 Government of Rajasthan, RUDSICO. 2017. *RUDSICO Human Resource Development Policy.* Jaipur. https://urban.rajasthan.gov. in/content/dam/raj/udh/organizations/ruidp/MISC/RUDSICO%20Human%20Resource%20Development%20Policy.pdf.

So others will not struggle as she did. As a young woman living in Jaisalmer, Kavita Kailash Khatri experienced the hardship of fetching water from distant sources. Later, as chair of the Jaisalmer Municipal Council, she found herself in a position to improve water availability for everyone in her city.

Damyanti Mahech grew up about 2 kilometers from Jaisalmer's rain-fed lake, in a community of about 15 families.

"Never did any men folk fetch water with us, but we liked to do it," she said, "First, because girls weren't allowed to go out of the house. So, collecting water was our chance. We got 1 hour in the morning to go out for water and 1 hour in the afternoon. Sometimes we would go in between."

It was also their chance to have some privacy. Without a toilet at home, they relied on safety in numbers when they used the nearby fields. They bathed once every 3 days or so, and fetched water for everyday household needs, but also to mix mud for smearing on the walls of the house to insulate it and repel mosquitos. Women carried the water in two brass pots on their heads, while younger girls carried only one.

Mahech was 12 years old when, in 1975, her community got its first water tap. The women would line up for an hour to wait their turn. If there was no more water by the time they reached the tap, they went back to the lake. Mahech did not appreciate the water tap very much. "I thought, 'Oh, now I won't get out of the house.' That was my favorite time of the day," she said. By this time in her life, she had already quit school. At 14 years of age, she became a wife. At 17, she became a mother. She has eight people living in her house, and 15 head of cattle down the street. Her family now gets more water than she has ever had in her life, and household suction pumps provide even more. Although illegal, she relies on her pumps to fill a 7,500-liter underground storage tank. In the summer, they purchase water from the city water tanker. She maintains a 1,000-liter tank for the cattle.

Mahech does not know how she ever got by as a young girl on so little water, or with so little education. "Now, we want our girls to study," she said. "I can't even imagine my daughters-in-law carrying water as I did, let alone my daughters and granddaughters."

Jaisalmer is a reminder of the fact that incremental development can be transformative. Over the years, community taps turned into household taps. Water used to be available for only one hour every 3 days, about 60–90 liters per capita per day, far less than the government's standard of 135 liters per capita per day. It came from the reservoir in the town of Mohangarh, 57 kilometers away. Then investments by the Asian Development Bank (ADB) ushered in a critical mass of urban infrastructure, specifically for water supplies, sewerage, drainage, and solid waste management.

continued on next page

More water for Jaisalmer. Damyanti Mahech, a resident of Jaisalmer, stores a total of 8,500 liters of water in two underground tanks, one for her family and a smaller one for their livestock. ADB investments in Jaisalmer have increased the city's water supply from 1 hour every 3 days to 1 hour daily. Meanwhile, the state government is investing in additional water supplies and coverage.

The investments in water supply infrastructure involved the overhaul of most of Jaisalmer's water system, including the construction or installation of: a new pumping station at Mohangarh reservoir, a transmission main into the city, raw water storage facilities, pump houses, a 7.7-kilometer rising main to improve water pressure, and an expanded network— all exceeding original design specifications. Households now receive 1 hour of water every day, compared with the 1 hour every 3 days before the project. The reservoir water is taken from the Indira Gandhi Canal, an economic lifeline that runs through Rajasthan.

The Government of Rajasthan, through the Rajasthan Urban Infrastructure Development Project (RUIDP), is making further investments in Jaisalmer, among them the installation of a new water transmission pipeline from the reservoir and the development of more networks and connections in the city. By replacing the old and leaking system, the city will be able to make water available for more hours every day. The state government is using the funds it was awarded by ADB for having accomplished a series of reforms outlined in a $250 million program loan. These funds could have been spent at the state government's discretion, but successful policy dialogues and RUIDP's own reassuring performance led the state government to approve the reinvestment of the funds in further urban development.

Jaisalmer will also pilot the corporatization of water supply management, which is currently under the aegis of Rajasthan's Public Health Engineering Department, as is the case in most cities throughout the state. Where ADB has invested, the treatment plants are privately managed, based on 5- to 10-year operation and maintenance contracts.

"If we can solve our water problems, it will be a big achievement for me," said Khatri, who has held public office since 2014.

When asked if she had ever imagined that the young woman who once carried pots of water on her head would one day be in a position to solve the entire city's water problems, she smiled, but quickly covered her mouth with her hand, shook her head, and closed her eyes. "No. I never imagined this," she said, as if in disbelief at how far both she and her city had come.

Source: Authors.

A Corporatized Utility to Manage Water Supply and Wastewater Services in Jaipur

Issue. Jaipur is Rajasthan's bustling capital, a major tourist destination for large numbers of foreign and domestic visitors, with a population of more than 3 million. The responsibilities for planning, developing, and operating the city's water and sewerage services were spread across multiple agencies, making coordination complicated and the services ineffectual.

Solution. The program loan enabled RUIDP to assist in the development of an independent corporatized water utility for Jaipur. The Jaipur Water Supply and Sewerage Board (JWSSB) has not yet been physically established. Once it is, the utility will manage water supply and wastewater services in the Jaipur metropolitan area. As is the general practice of modern public utilities, the board of directors adopted a business plan and human resource development policy.

Challenges. Once the state government approved the establishment of the new institutions (JWSSB and RUDSICO), one of RUIDP's biggest challenges was integrating traditional systems, practices, and decision-making processes into the newly reformed regime. Another major challenge was achieving synergy among the different working levels within JWSSB and RUDSICO, and between these institutions and other agencies—such as the Local Self Government Department, the Public Health Engineering Department (PHED), and the Directorate of Local Bodies. New work procedures had to be created, such as new sets of rules under the JWSSB Act, new staffing policies, and speedier decision-making processes within RUDSICO. Unionized employees expressed their opposition to the marginalization of institutions and to the new ways of doing business.

The key to addressing these challenges was to act collaboratively, yet decisively. The JWSSB staff would be drawn from other entities—the PHED, the Jaipur Development Authority (JDA), the Directorate of Local Bodies, and the Rajasthan Housing Board, among others—and a dedicated, skilled, professional cadre would be built for JWSSB and RUDSICO over time. New staff would eventually be added and trained by the existing deputed staff, enabling a smoother transition. RUIDP and the state government held frequent consultations with stakeholders, including union officials, to raise awareness about the people-friendly features of the new policies and the citizen-centric approach of both JWSSB and RUDSICO.

Phase 4 investments will provide technical support for the further strengthening of both of these new institutions.

State Water Supply Services Delegated to Municipalities

Issue. Constitutionally, ULBs are responsible for providing water services in urban areas. In practice, water services in Rajasthan are overseen by the state line agency PHED. This arrangement distances citizens (water customers) from the provider, and relieves the ULBs of responsibilities that directly affect the quality of life in their jurisdictions.

Solution. The program loan supports the devolution of assets and operations to the ULBs, thus increasing the ULBs' autonomy and their accountability to citizens.

Results. The state government has shifted water supply operations from the PHED to the ULBs in five RUIDP phase 3 towns whose projects include water supply components. RUIDP is supporting the ULBs during the state government's turnover of assets and in the development of the ULBs' capacity for operation and maintenance (O&M), given that the assets are now under the control of the municipalities, rather than the state. "ULBs need to remember that the public is depending on them to safeguard these important public assets, which RUIDP has implemented effectively on their behalf. Their capacity is limited, but it is growing," said Praveen Ankodia, deputy project director for RUIDP.

Other reforms, discussed below, support decentralization, the creation of additional revenue streams, and capacity-building programs.

Performance of Urban Water Utilities Benchmarked

Issue. The Finance Commission of India mandates that state governments require ULBs to publish performance-related data annually. It is an exercise in government accountability to the public, which government employees are either elected, appointed, or hired to serve. In reality, the ULBs and the state line agencies (such as the PHED) most deeply involved in RUIDP's work rarely have the capacity for this task, as it depends first and foremost on the availability of quality data, without which the entire exercise would have no integrity.

" PROJECT VOICES

ULBs need to remember that the public is depending on them to safeguard these important public assets, which RUIDP has implemented effectively on their behalf. Their capacity is limited, but it is growing.

Praveen Ankodia, deputy project director for RUIDP

Solutions. RUIDP is helping the state government establish a system for ULB data reporting related to the performance of their water supply and sanitation services. The system will be used to develop performance baselines and benchmarks, according to which the ULBs will be rated and ranked. The benchmarking program is a 5-year effort to generate quality data from all 31 ULBs that cover populations of more than 100,000, and to place the data in an online database for storage and analysis.

Challenges. The consulting team, led by Om Prakesh Goyal, a 35-year veteran of the PHED, from which he retired as a chief engineer, had to work with the ULBs, which were often uninformed, uncooperative, or unconvinced of the merits of benchmarking. The goal was to first generate the data, as the relevant data either did not exist or was unverifiable. The team includes 4 experts (one each for water supply, wastewater, finance, and information technology), 10 project consultants for collecting data from the PHED and the 31 ULBs, and 3 administrative staff members.

Benchmarking ULBs inherently promotes a better quality of urban governance. It brings greater transparency and accountability to the decisions that ULBs make about investments and service delivery at the local level. Good-quality data can help ULBs to better identify and prioritize needs and areas for investment, and it can highlight the strengths, weaknesses, and good practices among the ULBs, thereby generating healthy competition. It can also save money. As examples of the usefulness of data and benchmarking, Goyal pointed to a 2013 energy audit in Rajasthan that revealed that 50% of 900 pumping station examined, had an effectiveness rate of 30%–35%, against the norm of 60%–65%. Armed with this knowledge, decision makers knew which pumps to replace. Similarly, an audit of water trunk lines found that 50%–58% of the lines were leaking 30%–36% of the transmitted water. The audit made it possible to earmark the leakiest sections and prioritize funds for rehabilitation work. Conversely, audits of water distribution networks revealed that only 20 meters of pipelines needed to be replaced, rather than 60 meters, as previously thought.

"Unless the data is used for decision-making and for investment purposes, the ULBs won't take the benchmarking seriously," Goyal said. "It can't be seen as a formality. Otherwise, the data quality will be poor. But if ULBs see data result in additional grants, funds, and projects, then the data will be taken more seriously."

Results. The independent consulting team has prepared a user manual; developed data validation protocols; and established the baseline data systems, as well as an application for web-based data that is fully operational for all 31 ULBs. Performance data for every indicator for each ULB and across all ULBs can be accessed and compared. As of December 2019, the system was operational, and it may prove useful in supporting budget transfers. The Finance Commission of India mandates the linking of as much as 50% of funding allocations to performance benchmarks. The system will be turned over to the state government, and the benchmarking of ULB performance will continue, eventually expanding to all ULBs in the state.

Reforms to Improve Urban Governance

The program loan supported the rationalization of new or improved revenue streams for municipal services, alongside a set of new policies to guide long-term urban development. Water and sewerage services have been the beneficiaries of the financial reforms and new policies, some of which are among the first to be developed in the country. The utilities will benefit from an improved property tax system and higher, yet affordable tariffs, with annual increases guaranteed. The financial streams will help cover O&M expenses. New policies concerning urban development, urban water, and sewerage and wastewater are prioritizing investments and identifying the human resources needed to make cities in Rajasthan more livable.

Collecting Urban Property Taxes More Efficiently and Rationalizing Water Tariffs

Issue. A main reason for the underperformance of urban services is the lack of funding for O&M. The ability and willingness of ULBs to charge, bill, and collect sufficient water fees is essential for funding the O&M of systems, but charging the full cost is politically challenging. The revenues from drinking water services in Rajasthan is equivalent to just 20% of O&M costs.[28] The cost of the electricity needed to treat and distribute water supplies amounts to three times the revenues collected. Nearly 75% of the cost of producing each unit of water is subsidized. In most cities and towns, billing is based on average consumption, instead of metered use (60% of all connections are unmetered). In total, urban water supply services recover less than 40% of their costs.

Solutions. The state government has adopted and begun implementing new reforms that will enable the PHED to increasingly cover the cost of water supply service O&M by raising revenues through a combination of state transfers, taxation, and tariffs, as follows:

* transfers: sufficient state funds given to municipalities to ensure that minimum O&M is covered, beginning with the five RUIDP project towns selected for phase 3 that had water supply subprojects;
* taxation: an urban development tax based on reformed property tax rules; and
* tariffs: higher, yet affordable pro-poor tariff levels with annual increases of 10% for all customers.

Results. The reforms to financially stabilize urban water utilities in Rajasthan and make them sustainable are gaining traction, especially with regard to taxation and tariffs, as follows:

Urban development tax: To augment ULB revenues coming from state transfers and tariffs to cover the O&M expenses of water supply and sanitation systems, ADB and the state government agreed to improve the collection of the urban development tax.

The urban development tax is a tax on residential properties that are larger than 2,700 square feet. An independent audit confirmed that the state government, as stipulated in the program loan, collected the urban development tax on at least 50% of eligible properties from 50% of ULBs (95 of 190) for the financial years (FYs) 2017 (ended 31 March 2017) to 2019 (ended 31 March 2019). This policy incentivized municipalities to take advantage of the 74th Constitutional Amendment Act of the Government of India to strengthen resource mobilization at the local level.

---

[28] IFC. 2013. *Rajasthan Water Assessment: Potential for Private Sector Investments.* New Delhi.

Increased water tariffs: Based on a tariff study of various cities in Rajasthan, the state government developed a road map to guide utilities in raising tariffs to recover a minimum of 30% of O&M costs in 2017, with further annual increases until they could cover 100% of O&M expenses from the user tariffs. As part of the road map, the state government revised the tariff structure, with substantial increases in rates at the end of 2015, and a 10% increase every year thereafter. The new statewide tariff was the first change in water rates in more than 17 years, as the state government had never called for annual increases until this reform.

During phase 3, the five project towns with water supply components piloted the new tariff structure; and by FY2017, they had all recovered more than 30% of their water system O&M costs. In March 2017, the tariffs increased 10%, helping the utilities to recover more of their O&M costs. A few project cities are even posting revenue surpluses. These results have been confirmed in an independent study commissioned by the state government on the effects of the new water tariff structure. Efforts to promote the new tariff structure have also included ways to reduce costs and improve the efficiency of billing and collection.

Challenges. The new policies will not recover all of the costs of providing water and sewerage services, but revenues from water charges are growing.

ADB believes that the urban development tax could be more effective if the tax structure were revised to apply to all urban residential properties, as most are smaller than the current minimum of 2,700 square feet, and thus can escape the narrow tax net. ADB is advocating for the state government to reconsider an earlier proposal to broaden the tax net by eliminating or at least lowering the minimum square footage for eligibility.

"Going forward, the focus should increasingly be on improving cost recovery and ensuring that the willingness to charge is there, as people are generally willing to pay for an improved level of service," said Vivian Castro-Wooldridge, senior urban development specialist for ADB's South Asia Urban and Water Division and the former project officer for the RUIDP investments.

Financial sustainability is now required of ULBs, and a sector road map for sustainability will be included in the phase 4 investments.

Policies on Urban Development, Urban Water Supply, and Sewerage and Wastewater

Issue. The urban population in Rajasthan is rising steeply, currently constituting 24% of the total state population, along with a rise in number of towns. Large parts of Rajasthan are within the Delhi–Mumbai Industrial Corridor, which will stimulate substantially more urban growth. Due to the corridor, and increased state government investments, the proportion of Rajasthan's urban population is projected to rise to 40% by 2030. This rapid urbanization threatens to put a further strain on urban services and on economic growth.

Solutions. The state government has approved and adopted three policies: the Rajasthan Urban Development Policy, the Rajasthan Urban Water Supply Policy, and the State Sewerage and Wastewater Policy.

The first phase of implementation focused on building awareness within government departments and agencies about the policies and reforms that were likely to be developed and proposed. The initial awareness building required unexpected, significant efforts of coordination, especially at the local level, as well as more time than originally anticipated. Ultimately, the government entities whose buy-in for the policies was essential issued a joint letter of support to the state government.

The second phase of policy implementation was dedicated to research. RUIDP formed a committee of representatives to study service options that the policies could include, such as the district metered area approach, for achieving 24/7 water supplies and the corporatization of water utilities. ADB hosted study tours of the Dhaka Water and Sewerage Authority, which had successfully provided 24/7 water supplies, including to low-income neighborhoods.

Urban development policy: The Rajasthan Urban Development Policy provides a strategic framework for issues that are important for sustainable and equitable urban development: urban transport, urban water supply, wastewater management, stormwater drainage, solid waste management, affordable housing, slum redevelopment, urban governance, urban planning, inclusion and urban poverty, economic development and investments, eco-friendly cities, information and communication technology and smart cities, environment sustainability, and disaster resilience.[29] The policy provides a vision for cities in Rajasthan, includes long-term investment and financing plans, and indicates the critical reforms and infrastructure investments that should be prioritized.

Urban water policy: The state government approved the Rajasthan Urban Water Supply Policy in March 2018, augmenting the state's more general, sector-wide Rajasthan State Water Policy, 2010.[30] The Urban Water Supply Policy guides stakeholders—including government institutions, municipalities, water service providers, and water users—toward improving service efficiency and sustainability. It provides an overarching framework for addressing the legal, regulatory, institutional, administrative, and environmental issues and challenges faced by the urban water sector.

The key components of the policy are
* water supply service coverage, particularly individual water supply connections to households in slums and poor settlements;
* reduction of nonrevenue water;
* 24/7 water supplies;
* corporatization of water utilities;
* sustainable water management;
* capacity building and institutional strengthening; and
* an effective multilayer and multilevel grievance redressal mechanism.

29 Government of Rajasthan, Local Self Government Department. 2017. *Rajasthan: Urban Development Policy*. Jaipur. https://urban.rajasthan.gov.in/content/dam/raj/udh/organizations/ruidp/MISC/Rajasthan_Urban_Development_Policy_Final_Approved.pdf.

30 Government of Rajasthan, State Water Resource Planning Department. 2010. *State Water Policy*. Jaipur. https://www.indiawaterportal.org/sites/indiawaterportal.org/files/State%20Water%20Policy_%20State%20Water%20Resource%20Planning%20Department%20%28SWRPD%29_%20Government%20of%20Rajasthan_English%20version_2010.pdf.

Sewerage and wastewater policy: The state government approved the State Sewerage and Wastewater Policy in 2016; and in 2018 it approved the *Faecal Sludge & Septage Management Guidelines for Urban Rajasthan*—a pioneering policy for the country.[31] The guidelines are meant to support the Local Self Government Department and the ULBs in their efforts to end open defecation, improve public health, and protect the environment with an approach that will be affordable, technically feasible, and sustainable.

By 2021, an estimated 137 sewage treatment plants will serve nearly 60% of the total urban population in Rajasthan. A lower-cost, more sustainable system of fecal sludge and sewage management is a viable option for cities and towns that do not already have sewer networks, lack the financial capacity to support the O&M of traditional sewer systems and treatment plants, or are in areas where water is scarce. Phase 4 of the ADB–RUIDP investments will seek 100% sanitation coverage for fecal sludge and sewage management. House sewer connections will be included in the main civil works contracts, and the connection charges will not be passed on to the households. Design criteria for phase 4 investments include investments in sewerage systems only for the core areas with a sustainably sourced water supply capacity of at least 135 liters per capita per day, and a population density of more than 100 people per hectare. For all other urban areas, fecal sludge management (FSM) will be applied to achieve 100% urban sanitation coverage.

"The phase 4 investments in FSM as a sanitation option in Rajasthan is the largest effort of its kind in India to date, and is sure to provide great learning opportunities for many states in India and the region," said Castro-Wooldridge.

❝ PROJECT VOICES

The phase 4 investments in fecal sludge management as a sanitation option in Rajasthan is the largest effort of its kind in India to date, and is sure to provide great learning opportunities for many states in India and the region.

Vivian Castro-Wooldridge, senior urban development specialist for ADB's South Asia Urban and Water Division

---

31   Government of Rajasthan, Local Self Government Department. 2018. *Faecal Sludge & Septage Management Guidelines for Urban Rajasthan.* Jaipur. https://urban.rajasthan.gov.in/content/dam/raj/udh/organizations/ruidp/MISC/Final_State_FSSM_Guideline_upload.pdf.

Policy implementation and monitoring: The Rajasthan Urban Drinking Water, Sewerage & Infrastructure Corporation (RUDSICO) is the operational mechanism for implementing policies and reforms, while the PHED is responsible for the end-to-end management of water supply systems, including policy implementation, design, construction, O&M, billing and collection, and quality monitoring activities, for all system components (intake, treatment, transmission, and distribution). RUIDP is working with a training institute (Rajasthan State Institute of Public Administration) to develop the capacity of municipalities, especially for implementing policies and strengthening project management skills and O&M functions involving water supply and sanitation. In addition, the state government has formed two committees to monitor the implementation of its urban water supply, and sewerage and wastewater policies.

Capacity Building for Urban Development

The program loan supported the creation of a policy on human resource development for cities. A major feature of this policy was the establishment of the Centre for Urban Development in Rajasthan ("Rajasthan Shahari Vikas Kendra"), at the Rajasthan State Institute of Public Administration. The center is the state's mechanism for providing continuous training and education for the various stakeholder groups involved in the urban sector. Rajasthan is the first state in India to develop and approve a human resource development plan specifically for urban governance, and it is one of the few states to have a training institution solely for urban governance.

Policy on Human Resource Development for Cities

The state's new human resource development plan for urban governance calls for the training of 10,000 government employees, elected representatives, and experts in urban development from 2017 to 2021.[32] The establishment of the center signifies the state's seriousness about capacity building for urban development, governance, and planning. The policy has been instrumental in emphasizing human resources as a key input for improving urban governance.

The Goals of the Centre for Urban Development

The Centre for Urban Development is an independent, state-level training institute.[33] The objectives of the Centre, which is currently supported by the ADB program loan, include:
- developing and delivering training programs to 100% of ULB members by 2020; the trainings cover their functions, roles, and responsibilities in the context of urban reforms; and they are repeated for all newly elected ULB members;
- incorporating gender-responsive urban governance as a key training module;
- supporting the Local Self Government Department and ULBs in their development of service delivery norms, and conducting regular training programs to ensure their compliance with standards;
- studying urban sector and ULB reforms and documenting lessons learned; and
- conducting train-the-trainer programs to create a group of master trainers, thus enabling a speedy scaling up of instruction, as well as improved outreach.

---

[32] Government of Rajasthan, Local Self Government Department. 2017. *Human Resource Development Plan for Urban Governance in Rajasthan.* Jaipur. https://urban.rajasthan.gov.in/content/dam/raj/udh/organizations/ruidp/MISC/Human%20 Resource%20Development%20Plan%20for%20Urban%20Governance%20in%20Rajasthan%20-%20for%20upload.pdf.

[33] Rajasthan State Institute of Public Administration, Centre for Urban Development. http://www.hcmripa.gov.in/HSCRIPA1. aspx?mm=B+s/z7/+tIpxehJY01Wdlg==&m=Bg0B1b8w/9BeH6maTOXiaA==&s=7mWYgAE5B1Mkfb9nR8K8MA==.

Planners have to see the future in 20 years. The people in government can only see 5 years.

Reepunjaya Singh, professor of urban development at the Centre for Urban Development, Rajasthan State Institute of Public Administration

Challenges. One of the challenges of the center has been to move the horizon for all stakeholders to ensure that their capacity is keeping up with the pace of urban development. "Planners have to see the future in 20 years. The people in government can only see 5 years," said Reepunjaya Singh, the RUIDP focal point at the Centre for Urban Development, which is also based at the Rajasthan State Institute of Public Management.

Results. Since the Centre for Urban Development opened in May 2016, it has trained almost 4,000 urban government employees and elected public officials, who attended more than 75 sessions. Of those trained, 33.5% were women. The training sessions began with elected officials, then expanded to include engineers, architects, town planners, and administrators.

The center offers off-campus trainings that last 5 to 15 days. They take place around the state on an as-needed, as-requested, as-required basis. It also prepares and implements an annual training calendar, and documents good practices and lessons learned concerning the urban sector.

An independent agency carries out performance audits of the center, verifying that it has an adequate faculty in terms of size and expertise, as well as a sufficient budget for its operations.

Water relief. The construction of the Mansi Wakal Dam (a joint venture of Hindustan Zinc Ltd. and the Public Health and Engineering Department) applied standard engineering and construction methods to reduce the water deficit in Udaipur city and the local aquifers, also bringing relief to 22 villages in the city's surrounding tribal belt.

Preparing for the future, preserving the past.
A grandfather takes an evening stroll with his granddaughter in the plaza surrounding Jaipur's Ajmer Gate, which was renovated as part of the urban heritage work done by the ADB-financed RUIDP.

UNFINISHED BUSINESS

THE NEXT PHASE

Bird's-eye view. The western desert city of Jaisalmer in Rajasthan.

States and municipalities in India may find a model in what ADB, the state government, and RUIDP are achieving for Rajasthan's cities, which is based in equal parts on financing, technical capacity, institutional agility, visionary policy—and time. Despite what ADB and the state government have achieved through RUIDP, the sector reforms needed for the long-term sustainability of assets and improved services are still in their implementation infancy. Most ULBs have inadequate technical staff and own-source revenues for managing citywide water supplies and sanitation services. ULBs also have limited experience in the functions of water supply systems, smart water features, and the management and monitoring of contracts during O&M periods. This is true for ULBs that have been a part of the RUIDP investments, though to a much lesser extent than for ULBs that ADB support has yet to reach.

"Maturing all ULBs through the implementation of the sector reforms will be essential for scaling up the progress made during the first three investment phases. The development, approvals, and initial implementation of the sector reforms took about 7 years, but the real work of implementing and sustaining the reforms has only just begun," said current RUIDP Project Director Kumar Pal Gautam. Most of the towns in the state still need improved access to, and a better quality of, municipal services, especially water supply and sanitation. Rajasthan's scarce water resources must also be utilized more efficiently for long-term water security.

" PROJECT VOICES

... the real work of implementing and sustaining the reforms has only just begun.

Kumar Pal Gautam, current RUIDP project director

As the RUIDP investment teams have always done, the current team of ADB, the state government, and RUDSICO are addressing sustainability concerns and reform effectiveness by applying lessons from the past into the design of the next investment package, the Rajasthan Secondary Towns Development Sector Project, which is the fourth phase of ADB's urban investments in the state. However, phase 4 is the first part of a sector project encompassing a number of projects supporting smaller urban areas. And this sector project is part of the state government's 15-year sector development plan.

The sector development plan has been updated, and covers all the urban towns' infrastructure and non-infrastructure intervention requirements. The update expands the plan by including sanitation (not just water supplies), and the investment road map assumes that FSM will be implemented in conjunction with a sewerage system (in a departure from a sewerage-only approach). The plan also includes the approval of a new policy on FSM and asbestos reduction, the latter a new area of concern not discussed in this report. And the plan includes wastewater reuse guidelines.

The phase 4 investments have been designed to improve water supply services in secondary towns and heritage towns (14 such towns in the initial investment, with populations from 20,000 to 115,000). The design of this particular investment focuses on ensuring greater ownership by ULBs; on building their capacity and readiness to take over the assets from the state government; and on finding citywide sanitation solutions that will be more inclusive, cost-effective, and sustainable.

Previous project cities and towns will also benefit from phase 4 investments through the strengthening of sector reforms that were approved and rolled out during phase 3. The new institutions of RUDSICO, the Jaipur Water Supply and Sewerage Board (JWSSB), and the Centre for Urban Development will continue to receive ADB support (through project or technical assistance) for their contributions to the implementation of human resource development plans. Findings from the committees monitoring the implementation of the urban water supply and sewerage and wastewater policies will inform future policy work, and ADB will advocate for a similar committee to monitor the implementation of the urban development policy.

As the top body for urban development in Rajasthan, RUDSICO will undergo measures to strengthen its corporate governance, project development and management, and technical backstopping services to the ULBs. RUDSICO must meet the challenge of aligning the corporate systems and practices of the various urban entities (such as RUIDP) that contributed to its formation. This involves the difficult work of harmonizing financial systems, developing statewide project screening and appraisal procedures across all urban infrastructure sectors, and building an urban data center to gather and disseminate key urban performance data. ULBs, especially the smaller ones, need backstopping support for emergency repairs, financial planning, and monitoring and evaluation. RUDSICO, with its experienced army of RUIDP veterans, needs to serve as the water system support unit.

Taking Sustainability to the Next Level

The capacity of ULBs to operate and maintain their water supply systems (whether new investments turned over by RUIDP or existing ones) remains a priority. The RUIDP sector reforms have addressed the critical issue of sustainability from all angles—through policy entitlements, improved potential revenue streams, contractual arrangements with private operators, institutional development, and capacity building. ADB and the state government are planning to use the phase 4 investments to build on these initial steps and continue policy dialogues where consensus is still needed.

Issues and Solutions

The ULBs will remain dependent on insufficient state budget allocations if they do not take advantage of policies that would enable them to levy water tariffs, sewerage system user charges, and an urban development tax (based on property). If ULBs fail to utilize these revenue-generating options, the systems that the state government has borrowed money to build will not survive their initial lifetimes, as extending their durability would require certain levels of O&M and reinvestment. Moreover, proper O&M cannot happen without diverse revenue streams. These effective tariffs and other charges would also ensure that ULBs have adequate resources to pay contractors for their O&M services; otherwise, all operations would cease.

Water in the desert. ADB Bisalpur Dam is a gravity dam on the Banas River near Deoli in Tonk district, Rajasthan. The dam was completed in 1999 for the purpose of irrigation and water supply. Tonk, Jaipur, and Ajmer are the major towns of Rajasthan which are benefited with the water supply from this dam.

Tariffs. Tariffs are fundamental to sustainability, yet they are usually too low to sustain operations on their own. Sewerage tariffs are a surcharge on the water tariffs, ranging from 20% to 33%, and are collected along with the water bill by the PHED. As water tariffs are so low, even with the added sewerage surcharge, the revenues would still be inadequate for O&M cost recovery. Phase 4 proposes to increase sewerage charges. Some cities in South Asia, such as Dhaka, Bangladesh, have increased sewerage charges on a par with the charges for water supplies. Sewerage tariff reform is critical, given that sanitation investments are increasing exponentially in the region; also, O&M is typically much more expensive for sewerage systems than for water supply systems.[34]

More work will be needed to raise awareness among the ULBs, including their elected officials, of the consumers' willingness to pay for quality services. ADB is requiring the state government and ULBs in project cities to agree on ULB-based financial sustainability plans before project implementation, with clear indications as to how O&M costs will be met. Project towns will be required to develop implementation plans to meet their targets, with each plan specifying a road map of roles and responsibilities; the sources of funding for operational expenditures; and quantitative targets for cost reduction and improved financial and operational efficiency, which would be monitored throughout each project. With program loan funds, the state government will continue to support the Centre for Urban Development trainings for ULB staff, elected officials, and other stakeholders.

Taxes. As mentioned above, the tax base for the urban development tax is too narrow. As long as taxes are levied only on urban residential properties larger than 2,700 square feet, the urban development tax revenues will remain insufficient. Due to inadequate municipal revenues, the water supply systems and services will continue to suffer from inadequate O&M.

Policy dialogues between ADB and the state government should continue on the issue of property tax reform. ADB is advocating for the taxation of all urban residential properties, as this would widen the tax base considerably. A wider tax base is needed to secure the necessary revenues for the proper O&M of urban assets and services, especially for water supply systems.

Technical and managerial capacity. The design–build approach is now embedded in 10-year O&M contracts to ensure that the systems adhere to high standards of service quality, and that there is time to transfer the assets and functions to ULBs while retaining those high standards. However, experience with previous projects has shown that ULBs need (i) state and local commitments to increasing ULB staffing, (ii) more effort by RUDSICO to involve ULBs from the early stages, (iii) gap financing from the state for O&M, and (iv) more involvement by the state in the monitoring of O&M contracts. These forms of support would ensure that the ULBs of the project towns and cities will be ready for the handover.

---

[34] The O&M for sewerage systems is typically more expensive than that for water supply systems because they tend to require higher technology, more skilled staff, and higher power costs, though there are exceptions.

Phase 4 investments propose transfer plans and capacity building for ULBs to ensure that they are able to monitor the O&M contracts and that their staffs are large enough, properly trained, and involved. Capacity building includes establishment of a water supply cell within each ULB (with standard operating procedures), knowledge partnerships with stronger water operators, development and implementation of water safety plans, and establishment of effective billing and collection.

Continued institutional development. ULBs report that a lot of their own development is out of their control. For example, restrictive policies for hiring limit their recruitment, and thus their ability to manage existing and future assets and services. The state government is committed to increasing the staffs in the ULBs of each project town or city before construction commences. ULBs also report that policy and institutional responsibilities related to urban development are outside their control. RUDSICO should thus work with ULBs to identify the constraints and use related evidence to propose corrective measures that the state government could take to empower the ULBs.

Capacity building. Phase 4 will also see the continuation of awareness programs for students, elected officials, and ULB staff on issues related to water conservation, O&M, financial sustainability, climate change impacts, and public health (such as hygiene and the spread of communicable diseases). And phase 4 will continue to create new opportunities for women across the socioeconomic spectrum to develop their skills and participate in making their own communities more livable. Low-caste and indigenous women with limited economic opportunities can train to work as plumbers, meter readers, and valve operators, among other roles in project preparation, implementation, and monitoring.

Professional-track women will also have unprecedented opportunities through this project. To increase the number of women involved in urban development in the state, RUIDP proposes support for an internship program run by RUDSICO for female university students to gain professional experience in a technical field. "RUDSICO is really the premiere place for people to get experience on large urban infra projects in the state, but at the moment, the meeting rooms are filled with men: male government staff and male consultants. Our dream is that, as the result of this initiative, in a few years that imbalance will shift, and we'll see more women in decision-making and technical roles in the projects," said ADB's Vivian Castro-Wooldridge.

The holistic and comprehensive nature of the Livable Cities approach is evident in RUIDP's design and results. Castro-Wooldridge, who is overseeing ADB's phase 4 investments, said, "I have appreciated the RUIDP team's passion for their work and their willingness to increasingly look beyond asset development and push forward the agenda on gender, safeguards, financial sustainability, and strengthening of local government to ensure that a high quality of services can be sustained from the assets being created."

Cities in the Wake of COVID-19

Despite all the gains that this publication has presented, along with the lessons that RUIDP is still learning, the COVID-19 pandemic's impact on urban workers and residents, and on whole economies, exposes existing socioeconomic gaps, making them wider and more threatening than what was previously known or imagined. The importance of good governance and institutional capacity has been made more evident in the correlations being found between the crisis responses of the cities and the severity of the pandemic experienced.

With socioeconomic gaps being widened by COVID-19, there are opportunities for investment that could create better governed, more responsive, and more resilient urban societies. Water supplies and sanitation remain the essential frontline investments they have always been when it comes to strengthening public health, hygiene, and safety. They are now more urgent than ever. Ensuring that these systems are properly operated and maintained—and able to meet new demands during public health crises—will require deeper reforms to keep these systems financially viable, functional, and sustainable. And there should be accompanying infrastructure investments in capacity building to further the development of responsive governance and agile institutions.

COVID-19 has raised more questions than answers for leaders, thinkers, and designers in all sectors and levels of the global economy. The questions are important for inspiring new ways of viewing, designing, and reconstructing the post-COVID-19 city. Changes will be required to make cities more livable, especially under extraordinary circumstances like the COVID-19 lockdowns experienced by the majority of urban residents, none more so than the poor and other populations that are vulnerable to economic and social upheaval.

Rajasthan's story of urban development since 2000 is a good place to start for many urban leaders in India who are preparing for the challenges their cities will face after the COVID-19 pandemic is over.

RAJASTHAN URBAN INFRASTRUCTURE DEVELOPMENT PROJECT

DIRECTORS

		TENURE
1	Rajiv Swaroop	23 May 1998 to 15 July 2000
2	Vinod Kapoor	15 July 2000 to 23 August 2001
3	Manoj Sharma	23 August 2001 to 2 December 2004
4	Rohit Kumar Singh	2 December 2004 to 26 May 2006
5	Praveen Gupta	31 May 2006 to 26 October 2006
6	K.S. Rathore	26 October 2006 to 31 December 2008
7	Dinesh Kumar	1 January 2009 to 11 November 2009
8	R. Venkateswaran	12 November 2009 to 14 April 2010
9	Vaibhav Galriya	15 April 2010 to 22 June 2012
10	Pawan Kumar Goyal	22 June 2012 to 30 September 2012
11	Prithvi	3 October 2012 to 17 February 2014
12	Ambrish Kumar	25 February 2014 to 9 August 2014
13	Sudhansh Pant	9 August 2014 to 29 September 2014
14	Gayatri Rathore	1 October 2014 to 28 October 2014
15	Naveen Mahajan	10 November 2014 to 20 June 2016
16	Preetam B. Yashvant	27 June 2016 to 27 December 2018
17	Jitendra K. Soni	27 December 2018 to 5 July 2020
18	Kumar Pal Gautam	8 July 2020 to present

RUIDP = Rajasthan Urban Infrastructure Development Project.

Notes: The average tenure of an RUIDP project director is almost 16 months. There were 17 project directors over 22 years, with the longest tenure just over 3 years and 4 months, and the shortest about 1 month. The Government of Rajasthan has maintained project directors for relatively longer periods than is typical for directorships, thereby ensuring more stability and continuity, and minimizing disruptions in decision-making.

www.ingramcontent.com/pod-product-compliance
Lightning Source LLC
Chambersburg PA
CBHW050043220326
41599CB00045B/7270